THE SESAME STREET DICTIONARY

FEATURING

Jim Henson's Sesame Street Muppets

by Linda Hayward

illustrated by Joe Mathieu

Editor in Chief: Sharon Lerner

Art Directors: Grace Clarke and Cathy Goldsmith

With special thanks to Judith M. Leary

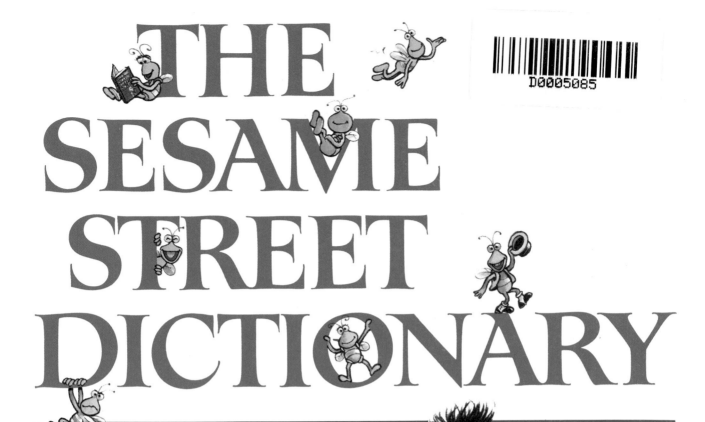

Random House/Children's Television Workshop

Since 1969 the *Sesame Street* television show has made learning an enjoyable and natural part of daily life for millions of children. *The Sesame Street Dictionary* fosters the same important educational goals. More than a standard beginner's dictionary, its many unique features make it a book with which a child can *grow* from age three to age eight. It has been carefully designed to be used in three stages:

- as a word book and vocabulary builder,
- as a reading-readiness storybook,
- as a first dictionary.

A primary goal of *The Sesame Street Dictionary* is to make using a dictionary an enjoyable as well as a rewarding experience. The exciting and humorous visual presentation invites the exploration of words and helps establish at an early age a positive attitude toward using dictionaries. Long before a child is old enough to read, he or she can *see* that this dictionary is fun. At the same time, *The Sesame Street Dictionary* provides accurate, complete, and easily understood information. More than 1,300 words are defined, illustrated, and used in context in one or more sample sentences.

The definitions are short, straightforward, and unusually clear and accurate. The vocabulary is structured for beginning readers. In all cases the definitions reflect the primary meaning of the word in terms of a child's world.

The word selection was based on several current vocabulary lists compiled by well-known educators. The dictionary concentrates on words that appear frequently in beginning reading books and in a young child's everyday world. Other words, such as *rocket, dinosaur,* and *skeleton,* were chosen because they fascinate children.

The lively, colorful illustrations reinforce and in many cases expand the definition of the word. For example, the verb *blow* is illustrated with four pictures in which a Muppet first blows *on* a trombone, then blows *up* a balloon, blows *away* bubbles, and finally blows *out* a birthday candle. This comic-strip-style flexibility gives the dictionary an exciting storybook appearance.

Children using this dictionary will quickly become familiar with the conventions used throughout. Amazing Mumford, the magician, pulls homonyms out of his hat, such as *bat* and *bat,* one being a baseball bat and the other a flying bat. A twiddlebug signals an exception or additional meaning. For example, one twiddlebug points out after the word *bean* that a jelly*bean* is only candy shaped like a *bean.* Each section closes with a humorous complaint from Oscar the Grouch. After the *R* section he asks "How can you have a dictionary without words like rude and rubbish and rotten?" A head word at the top of each page helps the child practice the use of alphabetization and prepares him or her for graduating into the longer, intermediate-grade dictionaries.

Games, riddles, and jokes are another unique feature of this book. These activities are used not only to reinforce word meanings but also to present educational concepts such as naming the parts of the body, counting, sorting objects by their characteristics, measuring, and relationships. Children who are familiar with the *Sesame Street* television show will delight in finding their favorite games from the show used in the dictionary. However, there is nothing about these games or anything else in the dictionary that requires knowledge of the television show.

The skillful integration of text and visual presentation results in a dictionary that is totally different from all other beginning dictionaries. Whether used as a word book with three- and four-year-olds, as a storybook with five- and six-year-olds, or as a useful dictionary with beginning readers, *The Sesame Street Dictionary* makes learning fun.

—Sharon Lerner,
Editor in Chief

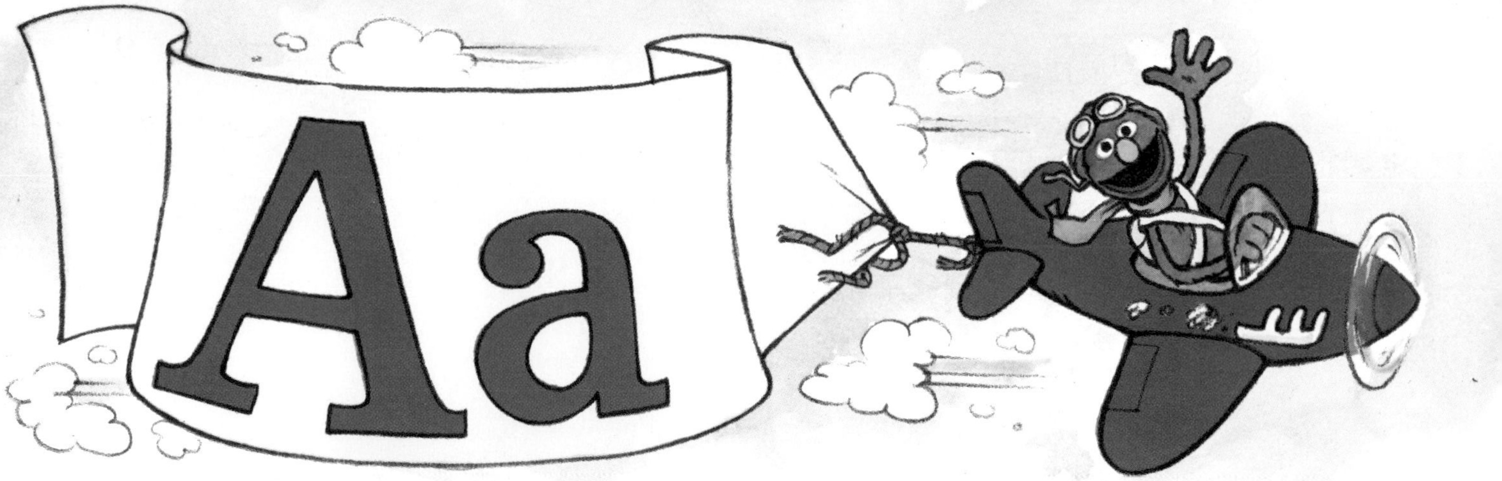

A B C D E F G H I J K L M N O P Q R S T U V W X Y Z

a A is a word that means one.

Bert is reaching for **a** book.

able When you are able to do something, you can do it.

Bert is **able** to reach the book. Ernie is not **able** to reach that high.

about About means on the subject of.

I wonder what this dictionary says **about** pigeons.

A dictionary is a book **about** words.

about About can also mean a little more or a little less or almost.

There are **about** thirteen hundred words in this dictionary.

above When you are above something, you are higher than it is.

Hello, everybod-ee! I, Grover, am flying my little airplane **above** the trees.

Uh-oh! Now I am *not* **above** the trees.

accident An accident is something that happens by mistake.

across When you go across something, you move from one side to the other side.

act When you act, you pretend to be someone or something else.

actor An actor is someone who acts.

Ernie and Bert are **actors.** They are acting in a play. The audience is watching them.

add When you add to something, you make it bigger.

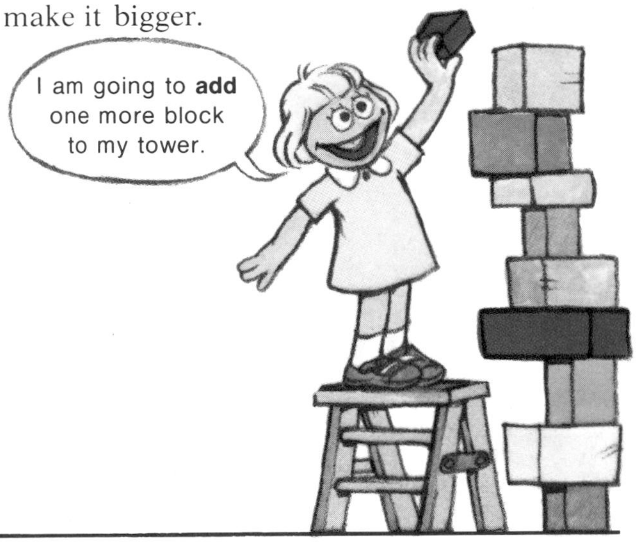

add When you add numbers or things, you find out how many there are all together.

address Your address is where you live.

Ernie and Bert live at 123 Sesame Street. 123 Sesame Street is their **address.**

adult An adult is someone who has grown up.

Our father, mother, and grandmother are the **adults** in our house.
My brother and I are the children.

adventure An adventure is something exciting that happens to someone.

afraid When you feel afraid, you are scared or frightened.

Don't be **afraid,** dear. Mommy is here.

Grover is **afraid** of the dark.

after After means later than.

Greetings! I am the Count! Do you know what I am doing? I am brushing my teeth.
And **after** I brush my teeth, I count them. One clean tooth, two clean teeth...

afternoon Afternoon is the time of the day that comes between morning and night.

Time for my **afternoon** snack!

again When you do something again, you do it one more time.

I'm Rodeo Rosie. And when I fall off a bucking bronco...
I get right back on **again!**

against Against means upon or touching.

against Against can also mean on opposite sides.

The Red Monster team is playing **against** the Blue Monster team.

age Your age is how old you are.

The Busby twins are the same **age.**

agree When people agree, they think the same way or want the same things.

The Busby twins **agree** about striped shirts.

ahead When you are ahead, you are in front.

The tortoise and the hare are having a race. The hare is **ahead.**

air Air is what you breathe. Air is all around you. It is what you feel when the wind blows.

airplane An airplane is something that you ride in. An airplane has wings and can move through the sky.

airport An airport is a place where airplanes take off and land.

Grover is landing his **airplane** at the **airport.**

alarm An alarm is a buzzer or a bell that wakes you or warns you.

The **alarm** on Big Bird's clock wakes him up.

The fire **alarm** warns the fire fighters that there is a fire.

alike When things are alike, they are the same.

The Busby twins look **alike.**

alive Things that are alive need food and water.

Plants are **alive.**

Animals are **alive.**

People are **alive.**

Rocks are not **alive.**

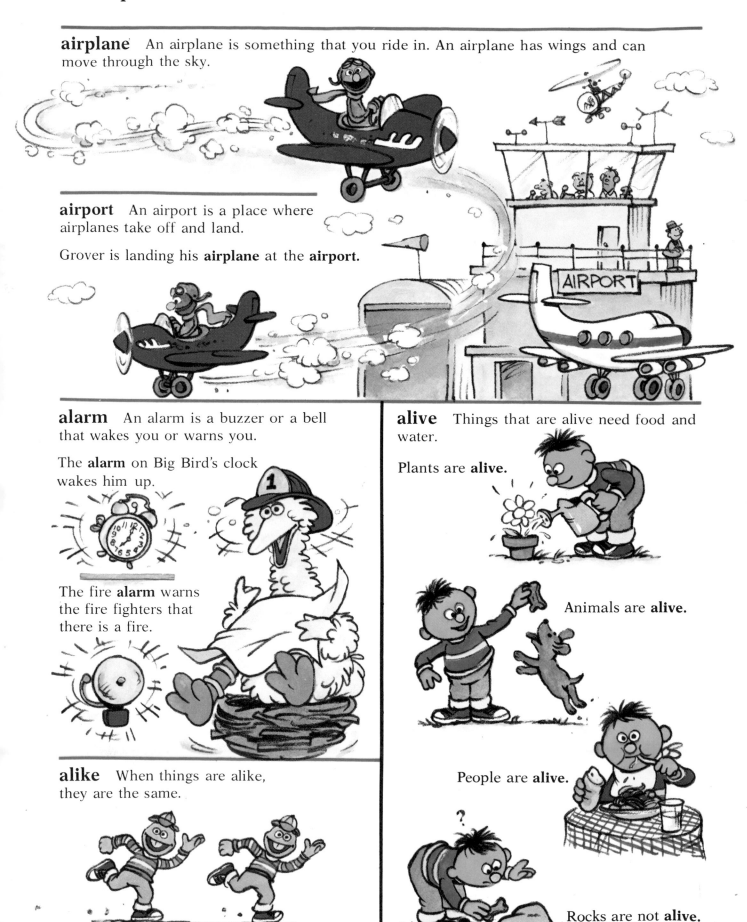

all All means everything with nothing left over.

Gee, Bert,
I don't know.
I guess you have
all the luck.
Ernie, why
am I carrying
all the groceries?

alligator An alligator is an animal with lots of teeth and a long tail.

Hi! My name is Prairie Dawn.
I wonder why most people
are afraid of **alligators.**

allow When you allow people to do something, you let them do it.

It has come to my
attention that some of you
are smiling. Well, smiling
is not **allowed.**
If you promise not to smile,
I will **allow** you to read
this dictionary.

almost Almost means nearly.

The cookies are **almost** gone.

alone When you are alone, no one is with you.

Hello again!
Remember me?
I am the Count and I love
to count things. When I am
alone, I count myself.
1...one Count!

along When you go along something, you move from one end toward the other end.

Sherlock Hemlock is walking **along** Sesame Street.

along Along can also mean together with.

Ernie took Rubber Duckie **along** with him.

aloud Aloud means loud enough to be heard, not in a whisper.

Big Bird likes to read **aloud.**

ABCDEFG...
HIJKLMNOP...
QRS...TUV...
WXYZ.
ALPHABET BOOK

alphabet The alphabet is all the letters from A to Z.

I, Sherlock Hemlock, the world's greatest detective, have discovered the world's longest word.
Oh, Sherlock! That's not a word. It's the **alphabet.**
A B C D E F G H I J K L M N O P Q R S T U V W X Y Z

Another way of saying **alphabet** is ABCs.

already Already means before now.

The Count is going to bed. He has **already** brushed his teeth.

also Also means too.

always Always means all the time or every time.

Cookie Monster has a big appetite. He is **always** hungry.

Ernie **always** has Rubber Duckie with him when he takes a bath.

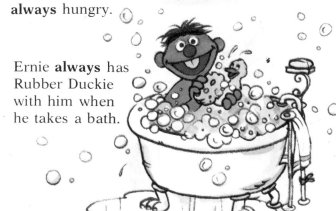

am Do you want to play WHO **AM** I?

I **am** Guy Smiley, star of daytime TV, here to play everybody's favorite game—WHO **AM** I?
WHO AM I?
I love to eat birdseed. Who **am** I?
I love to count birdseed. Who **am** I?
I love to find birdseed. Who **am** I?
I hate birdseed and I hate games. That is why I **am** hiding in my trash can.

among Among means in with or in the middle of.

Bert likes to walk **among** the pigeons.

among Among can also mean with some for each.

How do you divide four apples **among** five monsters?
You make applesauce.

amount Amount means how much or how many.

Now each one of us has the same **amount** of applesauce.

an An means one.

Grover is eating **an** apple.

and And means together with or also.

What is cute **and** lovable **and** blue **and** furry **and** goes up **and** down?
Grover the elevator operator!
1 2 3 4 5 6 7 8 9 10

angry When you get mad, you feel angry.

Ernie, please pick up these toys right away! This place is a mess!

Bert is **angry.**

animal An animal is any living thing that is not a plant. An animal can move from one place to another by itself. Most plants cannot.

Farmer Grover is feeding the **animals** on his farm.

another Another means one more.

I am picking a flower.

I am picking **another** flower. Now I have two flowers.

answer An answer is what you say to a question.

How much is one plus one?
The **answer** is two.

answer When you answer, you say something back.

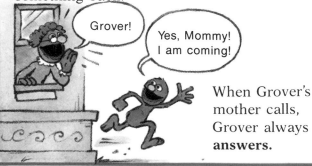

Grover!
Yes, Mommy! I am coming!

When Grover's mother calls, Grover always **answers.**

ant An ant is a small, crawling insect.

Look! The **ants** are taking my picnic lunch! Am I angry? No, I am happy. Now I can count them. 1, 2, 3, 4, 5... five wonderful **ants**!

any Any means one or some.

We grouches don't like **any**body or **any**one or **any**thing. Turn the page so I will not have to look at you **any**more.

apartment An apartment is a place to live in. There are many apartments in an apartment building.

Bert is playing the accordion in his **apartment.**

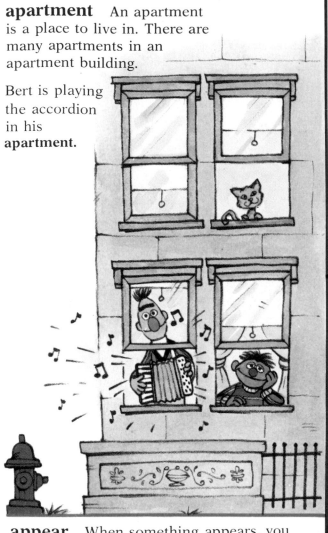

appear When something appears, you can see it.

I, the Amazing Mumford, will wave my magic wand and a rabbit will **appear.**
A LA PEANUT BUTTER SANDWICHES!
Now where is that rabbit?

apple An apple is a fruit that grows on an apple tree.

Here is my favorite thing that begins with A—**apple.**
And here is *my* favorite thing that begins with A—**apple** core.

are Big Bird and Snuffle-upagus **are** best friends.

You **are** my best friend, Mr. Snuffle-upagus.
You **are** *my* best friend, Bird.

arm Your arm is the part of your body between your shoulder and your hand.
Look up the word body.

around Around means in a circle.

Marshal Grover has a belt **around** his waist.

I have turned **around.** You cannot see my face.

artist An artist is someone who makes or does special things.

Some **artists** make pictures. Some **artists** make statues. Some **artists** dance. Some **artists** play musical instruments.

as As means equal to.

Big Bird is **as** tall **as** eight big blocks.

ask You ask a question when you want to find out the answer.

A detective has to **ask** many questions.

Who? What? Where? When? How? Why?

asleep When you are asleep, you are not awake.

I wonder if Bert is **asleep....** Oh, Bert. Are you **asleep**?
He doesn't hear me. I'll have to speak louder. HEY, BERT! ARE YOU **ASLEEP**?
zZZ
B
No, Ernie. You woke me up. I *was* **asleep.** Now I am awake.
B

astronaut An astronaut is someone who travels in a spaceship.

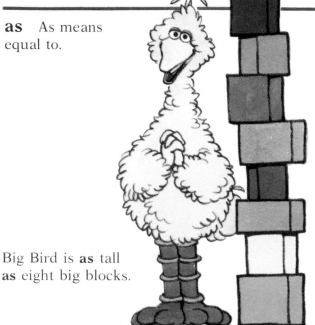

One small step for Grover Monster— one giant step for Monsterkind!

Grover the **astronaut** is on the moon.

at At tells when or where.

At night Little Bird likes to stay **at** home.

attention When you pay attention, you look and listen.

Herry Monster is not paying **attention.** He is bumping into everything.

aunt Your aunt is the sister of your mother or father.

AUNT ELMA
FATHER
Aunt Sally is my mother's sister. **Aunt** Elma is my father's sister.
AUNT SALLY
MOTHER
ME

author An author is someone who writes stories, poems, or plays.

Big Bird is the **author** of *Birds of a Feather.*

autumn Autumn is the name of a season. Autumn comes after summer. Another name for autumn is fall.

It must be **autumn.** The leaves are turning red and yellow.

awake When you are awake, you are not sleeping.

Bert is still **awake.**

away Away means somewhere else.

At last! This is the end of the A words. Now you can go **away** and leave me alone.

A **B** C D E F G H I J K L M N O P Q R S T U V W X Y Z

baby A baby is a very young child.

What do monsters have that nobody else has?
Baby monsters!

back Your back is the part of your body opposite your chest and between your neck and your hips. Look up the word body.

Prairie Dawn is hiking. She has a pack on her **back.**

back The back is also the part of a thing that is behind the front.

Grover's airplane has a propeller in front and a tail in **back.**

bad When something is bad, it is not good.

This is a **bad** day for a picnic.

When you feel bad, you don't feel good.

Bert has caught a cold. He feels **bad.**

Ernie is sorry that Bert is sick. Ernie feels **bad.**

bag A bag is a kind of container. You can put things in a bag.

bake When you bake something, you cook it in an oven.

baker A baker is someone who bakes.

bakery A bakery is the place where a baker bakes. A bakery is also a store where you can buy the things the baker bakes.

Everybody comes to Cookie's **bakery** to buy the cookies Cookie the **baker bakes.**

ball A ball is something to play with. Most balls are round.

balloon A balloon is a bag made of rubber. It can be filled with air or another kind of gas.

Prairie Dawn is blowing up a **balloon.**

banana A banana is a fruit that grows on banana trees.

band A band is a group of people playing musical instruments together.

What is blue and red and blue and makes music?
The Grover, Frazzle, and Cookie Monster Marching **Band**!

band A band is also a strip of material that goes around something.

Hey, Ernie, what can I use to hold my rubber **band** collection together?
How about a rubber **band,** Bert?

bank A bank is a place or thing to keep money in.

bank A bank is also the high ground along the side of a river.

I, the Amazing Mumford, will now pull from this perfectly empty hat two different things with the same name.
A LA PEANUT BUTTER SANDWICHES!

You see? Here is a piggy **bank.** But where is the other **bank**?
You are standing on it, Mumphie!

barber A barber is someone who cuts your hair.

Farley went to the **barber**shop. The **barber** cut Farley's hair.

bark A bark is a sound that a dog makes.

Barkley the dog can **bark** very loudly. The tree **bark** cannot.

bark Bark is also the outside covering of a tree.

barn A barn is a building on a farm where the farmer keeps cows, horses, hay, and grain.

Farmer Grover is going to his **barn** to milk his cows.

basket A basket is a kind of container. You can put things in a basket.

Here is my favorite **basket**— a picnic **basket** filled with apples and bananas and peanut butter sandwiches.
Here is *my* favorite **basket**— a waste**basket.** Just look at all this wonderful crumpled-up paper!

bat A bat is a small, furry animal that flies.

bat A bat is also a wooden stick. You can hit a ball with a bat.

I, the Amazing Mumford, will now pull from this perfectly empty hat two different things with the same name—
A LA PEANUT BUTTER SANDWICHES!

A baseball **bat** and a flying **bat.**

bath When you take a bath, you wash all over.

bathtub A bathtub is a thing in which you take a bath.

Ernie and Rubber Duckie are taking a **bath** in the **bathtub.**

be To be is to live or exist.

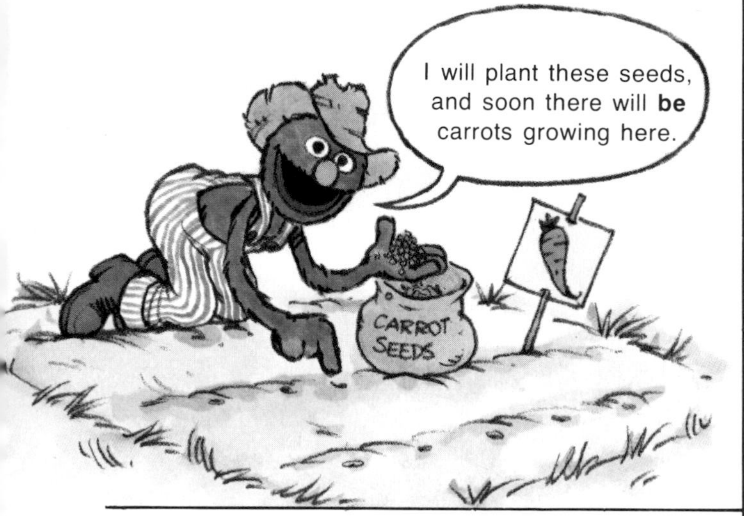
I will plant these seeds, and soon there will be carrots growing here.
CARROT SEEDS

beach A beach is the sandy or pebbly land next to an ocean, a lake, or a river.

Ernie and Bert are at the **beach.**

be Sometimes we use the word be to tell someone how to act.

Be careful not to step on my seeds!

bean A bean is a vegetable.

Here are some beans. They are all delicious.
string bean
kidney bean
lima bean
A jellybean is not a vegetable. It is a piece of candy shaped like a bean.
jellybean

bear A bear is a big, furry animal.

Once upon a time there were three **bears**—

beautiful When something you see or hear pleases you very much, you say it is beautiful.

because Because is a word that tells why.

bed A bed is a place to sleep.

bee A bee is a flying insect that buzzes. Some bees sting.

before Before is a word that means earlier than.

This is the chair **before** Herry Monster sat in it.

This is the chair after Herry Monster sat in it.

begin When you begin, you start.

beginning The beginning is the start of something.

Prairie Dawn always gets excited at the **beginning** of her favorite TV show.

behind When you are behind something, you are in back of it.

Farley is sitting **behind** Prairie Dawn. He wishes he were in front of her.

believe When you believe something, you think it is true.

Mr. Snuffle-upagus is real. But nobody **believes** me.
I **believe** you, Bird.

bell A bell is something that rings.

Roosevelt Franklin is ringing his bicycle **bell.**

Cookie Monster is ringing a door**bell.**

belong When something belongs to you, you own it.

Rubber Duckie **belongs** to Ernie.

belong When something belongs, it is in the right place.

Hey, Bert. Three of these things **belong** together. One of these things is not the same.
That's right, Ernie. That sock is a piece of clothing. The other things are toys. They **belong** in your toy box! What are they doing in my laundry basket?

below

When you are below something, you are lower than it is.

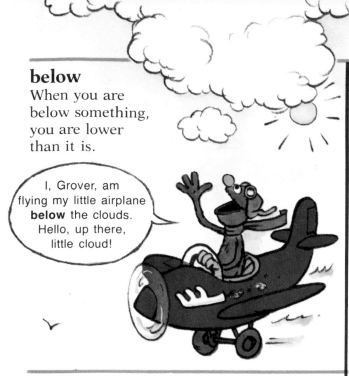

I, Grover, am flying my little airplane **below** the clouds. Hello, up there, little cloud!

beside

When you are beside something, you are next to it.

Herry Monster is standing **beside** the Busby twins.

between

When you are between two things, you are in the space that separates them.

Herry Monster is standing **between** the Busby twins.

bicycle

A bicycle is a machine that people ride. It has two wheels, handlebars, and pedals to make the wheels go around.

Grover likes to ride his **bicycle.**

Another name for a **bicycle** is bike.

big

Something big needs more room than something little. It is large, not small.

Big Bird needs a **big** nest.

Little Bird needs a little nest.

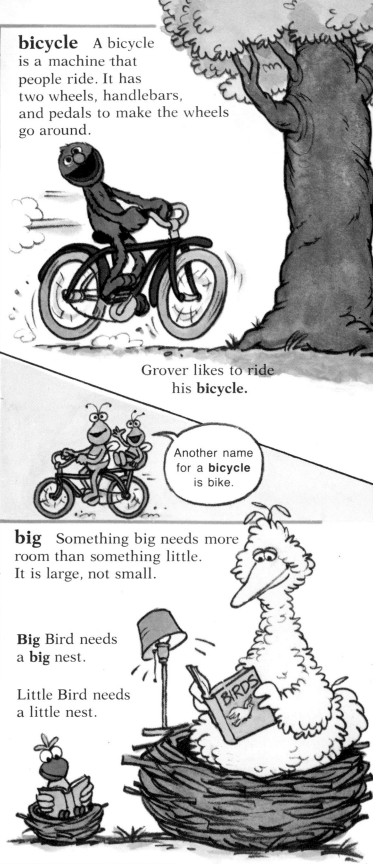

bird

A bird is an animal with feathers and a beak. Most birds can fly.

Big **Bird**'s feathers are yellow.

birthday Your birthday is the day of the year when you were born.

bite When you take a bite of something, you break off a piece with your teeth.

block A block is a building toy.

block A block is also a place for buildings in a town or city. Your block is your street from one corner to the other.

blood Blood is the red liquid that is pumped to all parts of your body by your heart. Blood flows through tubes called veins and arteries.

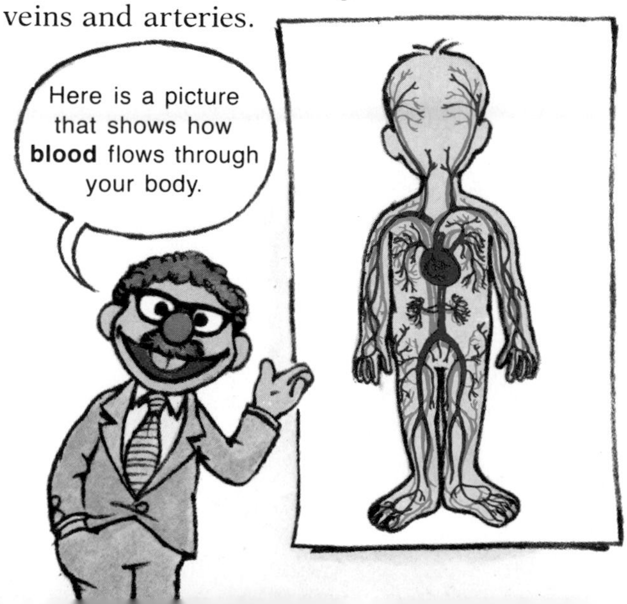

blow When you blow, air comes out of your mouth.

Here is something to **blow** on.

Here is something to **blow** up.

Here is something to **blow** away.

Here is something to **blow** out.

board A board is a flat piece of wood.

Bert has some **boards.**
He is going to build a birdhouse.

boat A boat is something that floats in the water and can carry people and things.

Some **boats** have sails.

Some **boats** have engines.

Some **boats** have oars.

Some **boats** have leaks.

body Your body is all of you, from the top of your head to the tips of your toes.

Can you name the parts of Bert's **body**?
hair
forehead
head
eyebrow
eye
cheek
ear
mouth
nose
chin
shoulder
neck
chest
back
arm
hip
stomach
bellybutton
wrist
hand
elbow
finger
knee
ankle
leg
toe
foot

bones A bone is a part of your body. Your bones are hard. Look up the word skeleton.

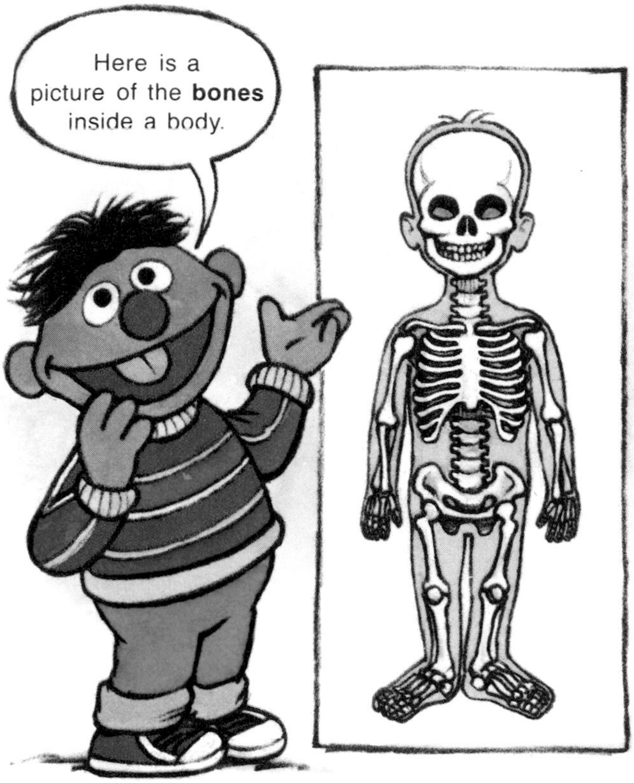

Here is a picture of the **bones** inside a body.

boot A boot is a shoe that covers the ankle.

Ernie is wearing red rain **boots** over his shoes.

Rodeo Rosie is wearing cowgirl **boots** instead of shoes.

born When a baby has grown big enough to be outside its mother's body, it is ready to be born.

This calf was just **born.**

book A book has sheets of paper between two covers. Most books have words. Some books have pictures.

This dictionary is a **book.**

both Both means two together.

Both Biff and Sully are eating lunch.

bottle A bottle is a kind of container, usually made of glass or plastic. A bottle can hold something that you pour.

Sully, pass me that **bottle** of Figgy Fizz, please.

bottom The bottom is the place farthest from the top.

bow A bow is a fancy knot. When you tie a bow, you make a knot with loops.

bow A bow is also a special kind of stick. It is used to play many stringed instruments.

bowl A bowl is a deep, round dish.

box A box is a kind of container. You can put things in a box.

boy A boy is a child who will grow up to be a man.

bread Bread is something to eat. It is made from flour and baked in an oven.

Three of these things belong together. One of these things is not the same.
white bread
French bread
rye bread
clock
The clock does not belong. You cannot eat a clock. But you can eat loaves of **bread.**

break When something breaks, it falls to pieces or stops working.

Oops! I did not mean to **break** the vase.

Ernie, stop playing with the television set or you'll **break** it. Then I won't be able to watch the Pigeon News.

breakfast Breakfast is the meal that you eat in the morning.

Bert has oatmeal for **breakfast** every day.

bridge A bridge is something that is built across water, roads, or deep valleys. People, cars, and other things can cross over a bridge.

123

The Count is driving his bat car over the **bridge.**

bring When you bring something, you have it with you when you come.

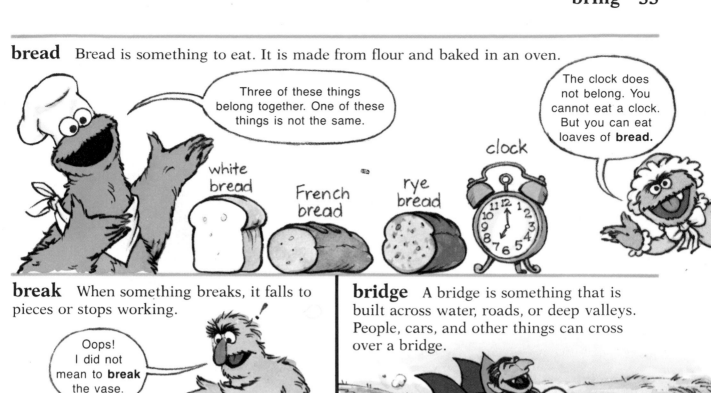

Big Bird, you didn't have to **bring** me a present.
I **brought** you a new vase.

broom A broom is a special kind of brush on the end of a long stick. It is used to sweep up dirt and trash.

Uh-oh! Herry Monster broke the new vase. Big Bird is using a **broom** to sweep up the pieces.

brother If your mother and father have another child who is a boy, he is your brother.

He is my **brother.**
She is my sister.

brush A brush is a tool made of bristles fastened to a handle.

Biff wants to paint the hallway. He has a can of paint. Which **brush** is better for Biff?

Sully wants to clean his teeth. He has some toothpaste. Which **brush** is better for Sully?

build When you build, you put pieces together to make something.

Bert is going to **build** a birdhouse.

Bert is **building** the birdhouse.

building A building is a place with walls and a roof.

Here is the **building** that Bert built. It is for the birds.

bump When you bump into something, you hit it with your body—usually by mistake.

bump A bump is a lump.

Watch out, Bert!
You will **bump**
your head.

Bert **bumped** into the birdhouse.

Now Bert has a **bump** on his head.

burn When something catches on fire, it burns. It gives out light and heat.

My candle has started to **burn.** Now I can see to count my pictures. But first, let me count my candle. 1... one candle!
1
2
3
Some things turn to ashes when they **burn.**

bus A bus is something that you ride in. It has lots of seats. A bus can carry many people from place to place.

SESAME STREET
READ BOOKS
Here comes the **bus**!
BUS STOP

Five people are waiting at the **bus** stop.

busy When you are busy, you have lots to do.

The bird watcher is **busy** watching birds.

The builder is **busy** building a building.

The bus driver is **busy** driving a bus.

The bricklayer is **busy** laying bricks.

but But means except.

Everyone is busy **but** Big Bird.

I feel like reading, but I don't have a book.
CAB

butcher A butcher is someone who cuts and sells meat for people to cook.

Herry Monster went to the **butcher** shop. He bought some meat from the **butcher**.

butterfly A butterfly is an insect with a thin body and four wings.

Catching a **butterfly** is not easy.

button A button is small and flat and usually round. Some buttons hold clothes together. Some buttons make things work.

Hey, Ernie, look at all the different **buttons** in my **button** collection.
Gee, Bert, you are missing the best **button** of all.

Which one is that?
The belly**button.** Heh! Heh!

Grover the elevator operator is pushing the **button** for the tenth floor.

buy When you buy something, you pay for it. After you buy something, it belongs to you.

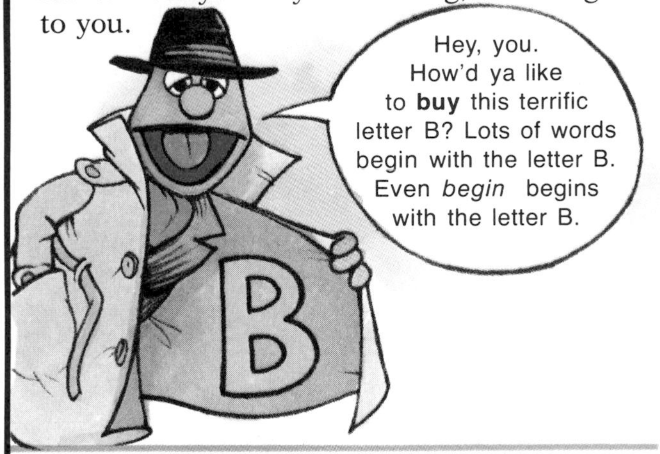
Hey, you. How'd ya like to **buy** this terrific letter B? Lots of words begin with the letter B. Even *begin* begins with the letter B.
B

by By means near or beside.

Oscar's garbage can is the one **by** the steps.

by If something was done by you, you did it.

I painted this picture all **by** myself.

These are supposed to be the B words, but I can't even find some of my favorite words that begin with B—words like bellyache, bothersome, blecch, and BEAT IT!

A B C D E F G H I J K L M N O P Q R S T U V W X Y Z

cake A cake is something sweet to eat. It is usually made with flour, eggs, butter, sugar, and other things.

Happy birthday, Grover! Me bake **cake** for you.
Thank you, Cookie Monster!
FLOUR

calendar A calendar tells you what day it is. It shows the months, weeks, and days of the year. There are seven days in a week and twelve months in a year.

The days of the week are Sunday, Monday, Tuesday, Wednesday, Thursday, Friday, and Saturday.

The months of the year are January, February, March, April, May, June, July, August, September, October, November, and December.

I can find my birthday on the **calendar.**

call When you call someone, you use a loud voice.

ERNIE!
You don't have to **call** me, Bert. I'm right here.

call When you call on a telephone, you use a telephone to speak to someone.

Hello, operator? I want to **call** my friend Mr. Snuffle-upagus.
Mr. Who?

can A can is a kind of container, usually made of metal. It is used to hold things.

Bert is opening a **can** of soup.

can When you can do something, it is possible for you to do it. You are able to do it.

Big Bird **can** reach the shelf.

Little Bird **can**not.

cap A cap is a kind of lid. It covers the top of something else.

Ernie just took the **cap** off a bottle of Figgy Fizz.

Ernie, save that bottle **cap**! I need it for my collection.

cap A cap is also something to wear on your head.

Bert is wearing a shower **cap.**

cape A cape is a coat without sleeves.

Super Grover wears a pink **cape.**

car A car is something that you ride in.

Some **cars** go on cables.
Some **cars** go on roads.
Some **cars** go on tracks.

card A card is a flat, stiff piece of paper. Often it has words and pictures on it.

Big Bird is making a birthday **card** for his friend Snuffle-upagus.

Rodeo Rosie and Bad Bart are playing a game with **cards.**

Go fish!

careful When you are careful, you pay attention to what you are doing.

I am **careful** when I cross the street.

carpenter A carpenter is someone who builds things with wood.

Bert the **carpenter** uses a saw to cut the wood. He uses a hammer to pound in the nails.

carpet A carpet is a cover for the floor.

Barkley likes to roll around on the **carpet.**

carrot A carrot is a vegetable. Carrots are orange and grow in the ground.

Farmer Grover is pulling up some **carrots** for dinner.

carry When you carry something, you pick it up and take it somewhere.

Herry Monster is very strong. He can **carry** a lot.

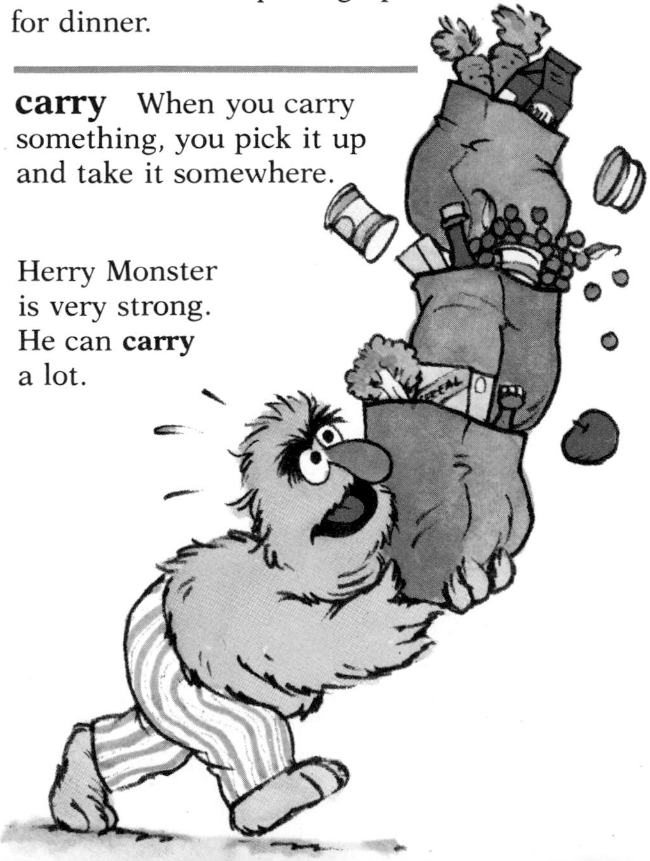

carton A carton is a kind of container. It can hold things.

Bert is carrying the groceries in a **carton.**

castle A castle is a very big building with tall towers and thick walls.

Come into my **castle.** But first let me count it. 1... one beautiful **castle**!

cat A cat is a furry animal with claws.

Some **cats** are small and tame.

Some **cats** are big and wild.

catch When you catch something, you grab it as it comes to you.

Ernie can **catch** a football.

When you **catch** a cold, you get sick.

cave A cave is a big hole under the ground or in the side of a hill.

Snuffle-upagus lives in a **cave.**

Snuffle-upagus

cent One cent is the smallest amount of money you can spend. If you have a penny, you have one cent. ← 1¢

A one-**cent** cookie costs a penny.

$0.01
1¢ COOKIES

ceiling The ceiling is the part of the room you see when you look up.

Prairie Dawn is painting the **ceiling.**

center The center is the place in the middle.

A doughnut has a hole in the **center.**

cereal Cereal is a food made from grain.

Ernie and Bert are eating **cereal** for breakfast. Bert is having oatmeal. Ernie is having crispies with milk.

certain When you are certain about something, you are very sure of it.

Are you **certain** that Cookie Monster will want this box of cookies?
Yes, I am sure he will.
COOKIES

chair A chair is a piece of furniture that you sit on. A chair has a back to lean against.

What time is it when Herry Monster sits on your **chair**?
Time to get a new **chair**!

change When you change something, you make it different.

I, the Amazing Mumford, will now **change** this cute little kitten into a big, ferocious lion!
A LA PEANUT BUTTER SANDWICHES!
Now I wonder how I can **change** this big, ferocious lion back into a cute little kitten!

chase When you chase something, you go after it.

Whoa, Fred! Wait for me!

Marshal Grover has to **chase** his horse, Fred.

cheek Your cheeks are the sides of your face. Look up the word face.

Roosevelt Franklin is kissing his mother on her **cheek.**

cheese Cheese is a food made from milk.

Prairie Dawn is having a picnic. She is eating **cheese** and crackers.

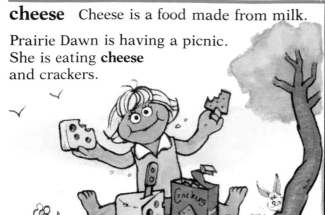

chest Your chest is the front part of your body between your neck and your stomach. Look up the word body.

The letter G is on Super Grover's **chest.**

chest A chest is also a kind of container. It is used to hold things.

Bert keeps his socks in a **chest** of drawers.

Herry Monster found a **chest** full of treasure.

chew When you chew, you mash up food with your teeth.

Fred likes to **chew** on a carrot.

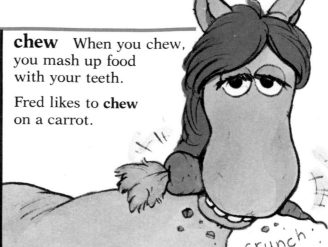

crunch

chicken A chicken is a kind of bird. Some chickens live on farms. Their eggs are good to eat.

I am a baby **chicken.** I am a chick.
I am the chick's father. I am a rooster.
I am the chick's mother. I am a hen.

child A child is a young boy or girl.

Charlie is the last **child** in line. There are three **children** in front of him.

chilly When you are chilly, you are too cool to be comfortable.

It is so cold
outside.
I am **chilly.**
I need my coat.

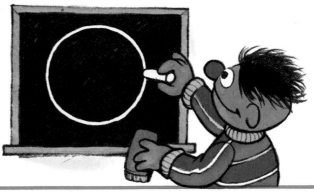

chin Your chin is the part of your face below your mouth. Look up the word face.

The Count has a beard on his **chin.**

choose When you choose, you pick one or the other.

Oh, Oscar! Which of these ice cream sundaes do you **choose**?
That's an easy **choice**! Is there anything better than cabbage ice cream with pickles and sardines?

circle A circle is a kind of shape. A circle is round.

Ernie is drawing a **circle** on the blackboard.

circus A circus is a special kind of show.

At the **circus** you can see clowns and acrobats and jugglers.

Circus animals do tricks.

city A city is a place where many people live and work.

Grover is flying his airplane over the **city.**

clean When something is clean, it is not dirty.

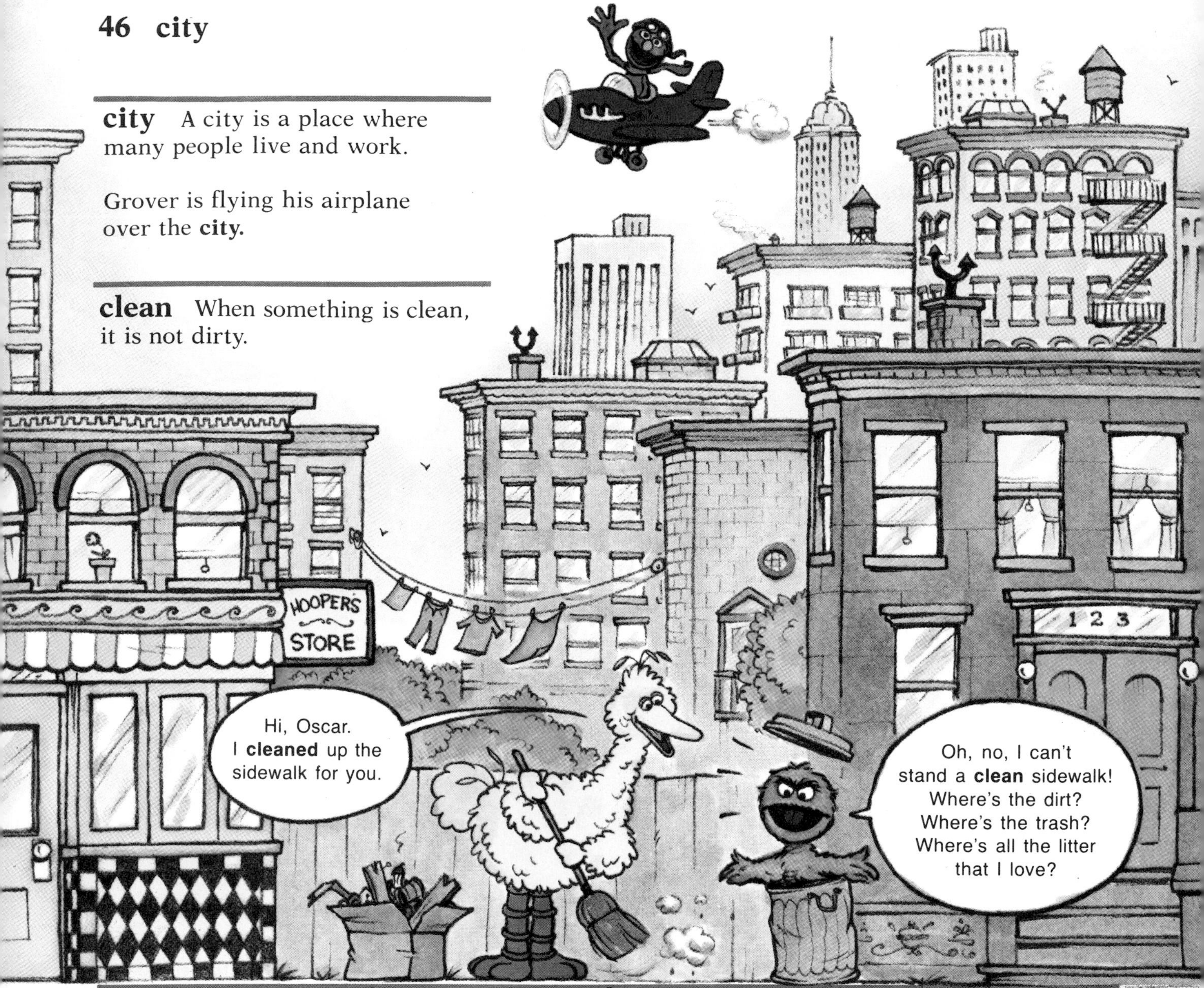
HOOPER'S STORE
Hi, Oscar.
I **cleaned** up the sidewalk for you.
Oh, no, I can't stand a **clean** sidewalk! Where's the dirt? Where's the trash? Where's all the litter that I love?
1 2 3

climb When you climb, you move up toward the top.

The Count has to **climb** up the tree to get his cat.

clock A clock is a kind of machine that shows you what time it is.

Hi!
I wonder why this **clock** is called a cuckoo **clock.**
PRESS
CUCKOO!
Oh!

close When you close something, you shut it.

Bert had to **close** the window.

AAGGH!
Oscar must be cooking stinkweed for dinner.

close When two things are close, they are near each other.

Oscar's trash can is **close** to Ernie and Bert's apartment.

closet A closet is a tiny room where you can keep things—especially clothes.

clothes Clothes are what people wear. Most clothes are made from cloth.

One of these things doesn't belong here.
I wonder what that horse is doing in my **closet** with my **clothes.**

cloud A cloud is made of tiny drops of water. Clouds float in the sky.

Grover can fly his airplane through a **cloud.**

coat A coat is a piece of clothing. You wear a coat over your other clothes.

The salesman has a letter C inside his **coat.**

coin A coin is a piece of money made from metal.

A penny, a nickel, a dime, and a quarter... four **coins**!

cold When the air is cold, you feel chilly.

It's **cold** outside, Ernie. You'd better wear a sweater or you might catch a **cold.**
When you catch a **cold,** you get sick.

collection A collection is a group of things that are alike in some way.

Hey, Ernie! Look at my paper clip **collection.**

color Color is all around us. The grass is green. The sky is blue. Red, yellow, orange, and purple are some of the other colors you see every day.

I, the Amazing Mumford, will now pull from this perfectly empty hat... one purple thing, one red thing, one blue thing, one yellow thing, one green thing, and one orange thing.
A LA PEANUT BUTTER SANDWICHES!

THING THING THING THING THING THING
Wow! Each thing is a different **color**!

come To come is to move from there to here.

Here I **come**! Hello, everybod-ee! I am still **coming.**
Here I go! Good-by, everybod-ee!
Grover **came,** but then he went away.

comfortable When you are comfortable, you feel good.

Big Bird is resting in his nest. He feels **comfortable.**

complain When you complain, you make a fuss about how things are.

Hey, everybody! Don't **complain**!
I can't breathe!
It's too hot!
Stop wiggling!
It's too crowded!
Stop poking!

container A container is something that can hold something else. There are many kinds of containers.

FIND YOUR CONTAINER!
And now—the game show everyone has been waiting for—FIND YOUR **CONTAINER**! As you know, each week our contestants come on stage with their favorite things. Each of them has to find a **container** to put them in.
TRASH
Cookies
TOYS

cook When you cook, you use heat to prepare food to eat.

cook A cook is someone who cooks.

My dad likes to **cook** spaghetti. He is a good **cook.**

cookie A cookie is something to eat. It is usually small, flat, and sweet.

Cookies are **Cookie** Monster's favorite food.

C is for **Cookie.** That's good enough for me.

cool When something feels cool, it is more cold than hot.

Cookies!
They are too hot. Wait until they are **cool**!

cooperate When you cooperate, you work together with someone to do something.

Fire fighters have to **cooperate** to put out a fire.

corner A corner is the point where two sides come together.

The **corner** of a room is the place where one wall meets another.

The **corner** of a triangle is the place where one line meets another.

A **corner** is also the place where two streets meet.

Bert was supposed to meet me at this **corner.**
EDEN
GROVE
WALK

costume A costume is something to wear. It can help you pretend to be someone else.

Grover's mommy made him a Halloween **costume.**

Just what I wanted—
a superhero **costume**!
Thank you, Mommy!

count When you count, you say numbers in order. Counting can help you find out how many things there are all together.

Here are my pet bats.
How many do I have?
Let us **count** them.
1, 2, 3, 4, 5, 6, 7, 8, 9 ...
nine bats!

country A country is a place where many people live. Some countries are large. Some are small.

The United States
of America is
a large **country.**

country Country is also a name for a place that is not like the city. In the country there is usually a lot of grass and trees, but not many buildings.

I live
in the **country.**
I see cows and horses
and ducks and a few
small buildings.

I live in the city.
I see cars and buses
and trucks and many
big buildings.
TAXI
TAXI

cousin The child of your aunt and uncle is your cousin.

me
my cousin Carol
my aunt Genevieve
my uncle Fred

cover When you cover people or things, you put something over them.

Ernie likes to **cover** Bert with sand at the beach.

cow A cow is an animal that usually lives on a farm and gives milk.

I am a baby **cow.** I am a calf.
I am the calf's mother. I am a **cow.**
I am the calf's father. I am a bull.

crab A crab is an animal that lives in or near the water. A crab has a hard shell, eight legs, and two claws.

I have always wondered why **crabs** have such big claws.
Ow! Now I know!

crack When something cracks, it starts to break.

Uh-oh! My wing is beginning to **crack.**

crash When one thing hits another with a loud noise, it crashes.

I am going to **crash.**
CRASH!

crawl When you crawl, you move on your hands and your knees.

It is not easy being Grover.

Grover has to **crawl** out of his airplane.

crayon A crayon is a stick of colored wax used to draw on paper.

I have a new box of **crayons.** I am drawing a picture of my friend Mr. Snuffle-upagus.
CRAYONS

cream Cream is the thick part of milk that is made into butter.

I am churning the **cream** to make butter.
Another thing you can make from **cream** is ice **cream**!

cross When you cross something, you go from one side of it to the other.

You should always look both ways before you **cross** the street.

crowd A crowd is a lot of people together.

A **crowd** is waiting for a bus.

There is already a **crowd** on the bus.

cry When you cry, tears come from your eyes.

Grover spilled his milk and began to **cry.**

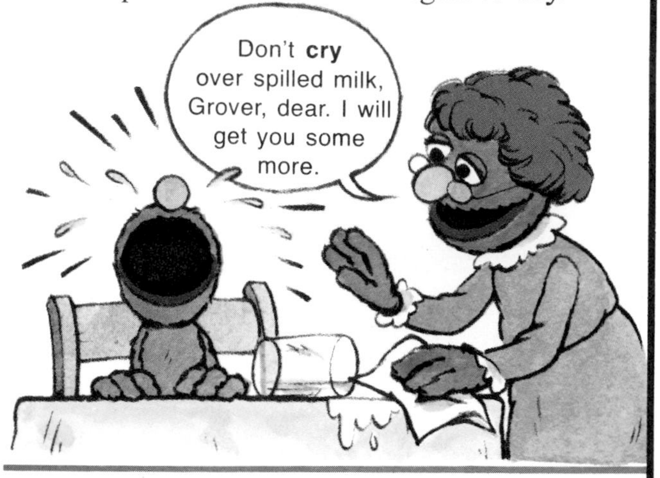
Don't **cry** over spilled milk, Grover, dear. I will get you some more.

cup A cup is a container to drink from. Usually it has a handle.

Snuffle-upagus has a very large **cup.**

curious When you are curious, you wonder about something.

I wonder who lives in this cave.

Prairie Dawn is **curious.**

cut When you cut something, you divide it into pieces. Most often you use scissors or a knife.

Big Bird can **cut** out paper dolls with scissors.

Cookie the baker **cuts** his cookie dough with a knife.

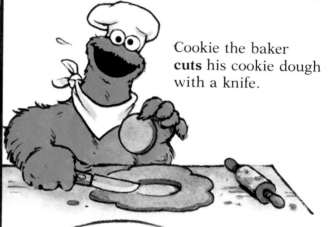

I have a complaint! Why were all the wonderful words that begin with C left out of this dictionary? Where are my favorites, like crabby and creepy? What happened to chipped and crumpled? This is a crummy dictionary.

A B C D E F G H I J K L M N O P Q R S T U V W X Y Z

dance When you dance, you move with rhythm. Usually you dance to music.

dancer A dancer is someone who dances.

The piper is piping. The **dancer** is **dancing.**

danger If there is danger, there is a chance that someone may get hurt.

There is a **danger** sign. I should be careful.
DANGER

dark When it is dark, there is no light.

It is so **dark** in here. But I am not afraid. I have my teddy bear.

date The date is the day, month, and year when something happens.

The date George Washington became the first President is April 30, 1789.

daughter A girl or a woman is the daughter of her mother and father.

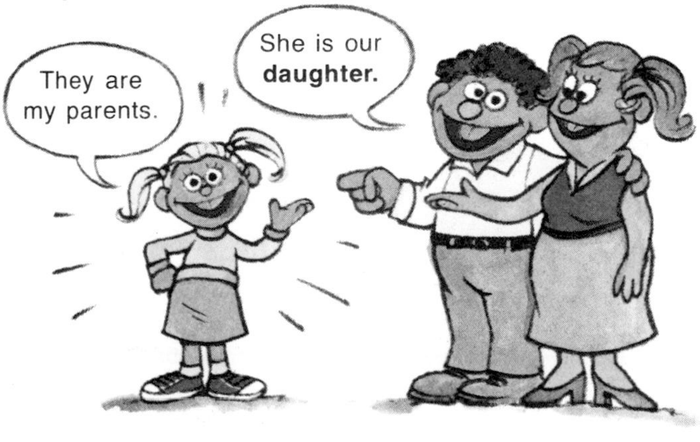
They are my parents.
She is our **daughter.**

dawn Dawn is the time when the sun begins to light up the sky.

Farmer Grover's rooster crows at **dawn.** It is time for Farmer Grover to wake up.

day A day is twenty-four hours long. Morning, afternoon, and night are all parts of a day.

Each **day** I wake up in the morning.
During the afternoon I eat birdseed...
and play games with my friend Mr. Snuffle-upagus....
At night I go to sleep.
Sometimes people use the word **day** to mean the opposite of night.

deaf A person who is deaf cannot hear.

If you know sign language, you can talk to a **deaf** person with your hands.

I
love
you.

decide When you decide, you make up your mind.

Cookie Monster cannot **decide** what to eat.

Me want chocolate-chip cookie. But oatmeal-raisin cookie look delicious, too.
?

Cookie Monster **decided** to eat both.

YUM!

decorate When you decorate something, you make it pretty.

Cookie the baker is going to **decorate** a cake.

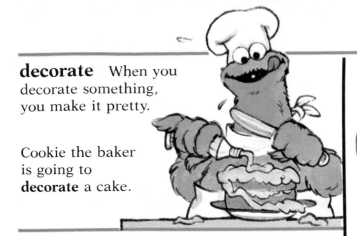

deep When something is deep, the bottom is far below the top.

I, Grover, am standing in **deep** water.
Now I am in **deeper** water.
This is the **deepest** part of the —
GLUB
GLUB
GLUB...

deer A deer is an animal with four legs. Most deer live in the forest. The father deer has antlers on his head.

I am a baby **deer.** I am a fawn.
I am the fawn's father. I am a buck.
I am the fawn's mother. I am a doe.

delicious When food is delicious, it tastes good.

Delicious!

deliver When you deliver something, you take it to a place or person.

I'm the Mudman. I'm here to **deliver** mud to Oscar.
MUDMAN
Delivery

dentist A dentist is someone who helps you take care of your teeth.

The **dentist** is counting and cleaning Farley's teeth.

describe When you describe people or things, you tell about them.

Super Grover is fast.
Super Grover is smart.
1+1=2
Super Grover is brave.
And I am cute, too.

Fast, smart, brave, and cute are words that **describe** Super Grover.

desert A desert is a place with very little water. Most deserts are covered with sand.

1 ... one
cactus plant,
2 ... two
cactus plants ...

Cactus plants can grow in the **desert** because they do not need much water.

desk A desk is a special table where you can write or draw.

Farley is sitting at his **desk** and writing a letter.

dessert A dessert is a special food that you eat at the end of a meal.

Cookie Monster is having cookies for **dessert.**

detective A detective is someone who tries to find the answer to a mystery.

Sherlock Hemlock is a **detective.** He is looking for clues.

dictionary A dictionary is a book that tells the meanings of words.

This book is a **dictionary.**

Hey, Ernie,
listen to this.
The **dictionary** says
that oatmeal is a
kind of cereal
made from oats.
Very
interesting,
Bert.

die When things die, they stop living.

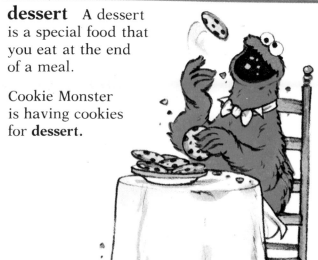

Fall is here.
Soon all the
leaves will **die.**
The leaves on
the ground
are **dead.**

different When things are different, they are not the same.

Big Bird is big.
Little Bird is small.
Big Bird and Little Bird are **different** sizes.

difficult When something is difficult, it is hard to do.

It is **difficult** for Big Bird to fit into a phone booth.

dig When you dig in the ground, you scoop up dirt.

Barkley likes to **dig** holes. He has already **dug** three.

dime A dime is a coin. A dime is equal to ten cents. Look up the word coin.

I have a **dime.**
I have ten pennies.

Each of the Busby twins has ten cents.

dinner Dinner is usually the biggest meal of the day.

Cookie Monster has a well-balanced **dinner.**

dinosaur A dinosaur is a kind of animal that lived millions of years ago.

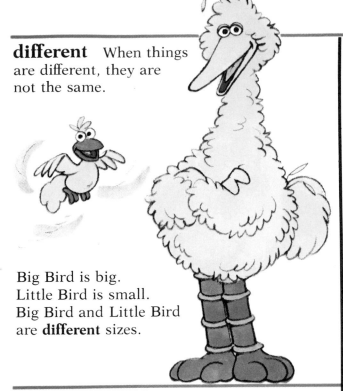

Some **dinosaurs** were bigger than houses. I'm glad there are no **dinosaurs** alive today.

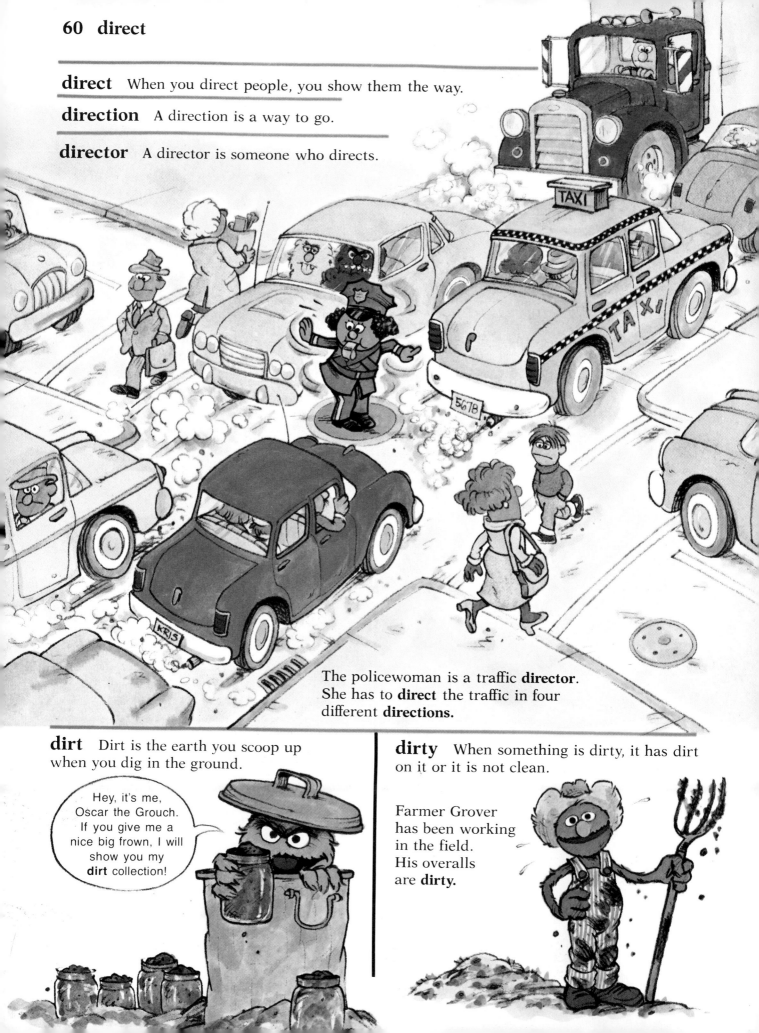

direct When you direct people, you show them the way.

direction A direction is a way to go.

director A director is someone who directs.

The policewoman is a traffic **director**. She has to **direct** the traffic in four different **directions.**

dirt Dirt is the earth you scoop up when you dig in the ground.

Hey, it's me, Oscar the Grouch. If you give me a nice big frown, I will show you my **dirt** collection!

dirty When something is dirty, it has dirt on it or it is not clean.

Farmer Grover has been working in the field. His overalls are **dirty.**

disagree When people disagree, they want different things or their ideas are not the same.

I want to go up.
I want to go down.

The Busby twins **disagree.**

disappear When something disappears, you cannot see it anymore.

I, the Amazing Mumford, will now wave my magic wand and make this rabbit **disappear.**
A LA PEANUT BUTTER SANDWICHES!

What happened to Mumphie? He **disappeared.**

disappointed You feel disappointed when something you want to happen does not happen.

Big Bird did not find any mail in his mailbox. He was **disappointed.**

BIG BIRD

discover When you discover something, you find it.

Zounds! Two suspicious-looking feet. I must **discover** whose they are.

disguise You wear a disguise to look like something or someone else.

The Big Bad Wolf is wearing a **disguise** to look like Grandma.

dish A dish is a kind of container to hold food.

Frazzle is taking a **dish** out of the cupboard.

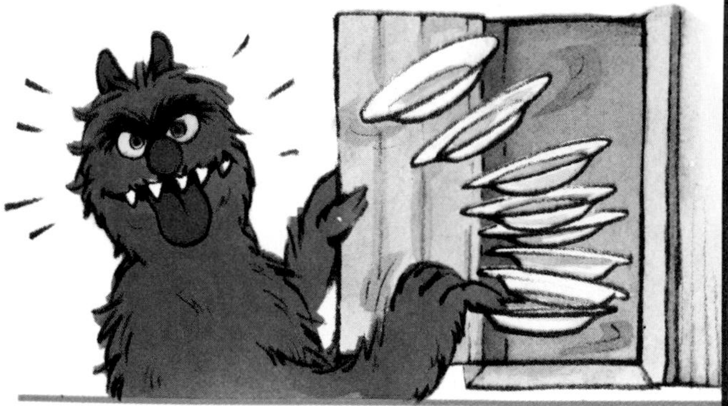

distance Distance is the amount of space between two places or things.

The **distance** from Oscar's mud box to the fire hydrant is six feet.

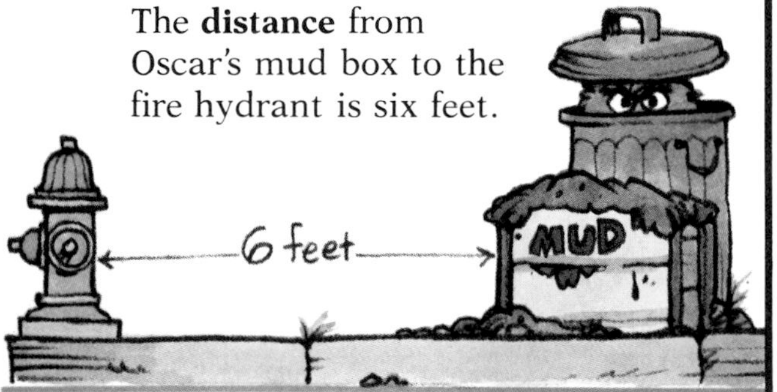
6 feet
MUD

divide When you divide something, you separate it into parts.

Ernie, I will **divide** this apple into two parts so that you can have half and I can have half.

Bert, I think you should have **divided** that apple into three parts.

do When you do something, you act in a certain way or you make something happen.

Every Thursday, I **do** my house-messing. When it gets too neat around here, I have to mess things up.

doctor A doctor is someone who helps people stay healthy. Doctors also help sick people get well.

The **doctor** is listening to Farley's heart with a stethoscope.

dog A dog is a kind of furry animal with a tail. Most dogs bark.

One of these things does not belong here.

A collie, a dachshund, and a poodle are all **dogs.** A turkey is a bird. The turkey does not belong.

doll A doll is a toy that looks like a person.

Herry Monster's **doll** has red hair.

dollar A dollar is an amount of money. A dollar bill is a piece of paper money equal to one hundred cents.

I, the Amazing Mumford, will now change one hundred pennies into a **dollar** bill.
Here are one hundred pennies.
Here's a **dollar.**
That's no trick! Anyone can trade a hundred pennies for a **dollar** bill.

done When something is done, it is finished.

My house-messing is **done.** Now I won't have to mess up my can until next Thursday.
MUD

door A door is used to close off the way into something.

Herry Monster, do you know how to open a **door**?
Sure.
CRUNCH!

doorknob A doorknob is a handle on a door.

No, no, Herry Monster! You are supposed to turn the **doorknob** when you open a door.
CRUNCH!
?

dot A dot is a very tiny round mark.

Sherlock Hemlock is looking at a **dot** on a piece of paper through his magnifying glass.

CLUE FOR THE DAY

double When something is double, there are two instead of one.

ICE CREAM
Grover the ice cream vendor gave me a **double** scoop of ice cream.

down When you go down, you move to a lower place.

Bert is going **down** the steps.

dozen When you have twelve things, you have a dozen of them.

12
Look! I have a **dozen** eggs! Will I fry them or scramble them? No! I will count them.

dragon A dragon is an imaginary animal that has wings and breathes fire.

Roosevelt Franklin is reading a book about a **dragon.**

draw When you draw, you make a picture. You can draw with a pencil or a pen or a crayon.

Roosevelt Franklin can **draw** a picture of a dragon.

drawer A drawer is a kind of container that slides in and out of a piece of furniture. You can keep things in a drawer.

Bert is folding his socks and putting them into his **drawer.**

dream When you dream, you see, think, and feel things while you sleep.

Cookie Monster likes to **dream** about his favorite thing.

dress A dress is something to wear.

Betty Lou is putting on a **dress.**

dress When you dress, you put on clothes.

I am so proud. I can **dress** myself.

drink When you drink, you swallow a liquid.

I love to **drink** orange juice.
I love to **drink** pickle juice.

drive When you drive something, you make it go and steer it.

driver The driver is the one who is driving.

Grover Knover can **drive** his motorcycle over ten barrels. Grover Knover is a good **driver.**

drop A drop is a small amount of liquid.

Sherlock Hemlock is looking at a **drop** of rain.

drop When you drop something, you let it fall.

I, Grover, the flying letter carrier, will **drop** the mail to my friends on Sesame Street.
U.S. MAIL

drum A drum is a musical instrument. When you play a drum, you hit it with your hands or with drumsticks.

Ernie is playing the **drum**.

dry When something is dry, it is not wet.

It is raining, but my little umbrella keeps me **dry**.
Now I am all wet. Next time I will wear my raincoat.

dry When you dry something, you take away the water.

Biff likes to wash the dishes. Sully likes to **dry** them.

duck A duck is a kind of bird. Ducks have webbed feet. Ducks can fly or walk or swim.

I am the **duck**ling's father. I am a drake.
I am a baby **duck.** I am a **duck**ling.
I am the **duck**ling's mother. I am a **duck.**

Farmer Grover's **ducks** are swimming in the pond.

duckie A duckie is a toy duck.

Rubber **Duckie** is a toy that floats in Ernie's bathtub.

dump The dump is a place for garbage.

dump When you dump something, you get rid of it.

I love to visit the **dump**! It is one of my favorite places.

The garbage truck takes the garbage to the **dump** to **dump** it.

during During is a word that means between the beginning and the end.

We are about to begin our show. **During** the show, everyone must be quiet.

dust Dust is very small bits of dirt.

Dirt! Dump! **Dust!** This is not such a dumb dictionary after all.

Oscar loves to have **dust** in his can.

A B C D E F G H I J K L M N O P Q R S T U V W X Y Z

each Each means every or every one.

ear Your ear is the part of your body that you use for hearing. Look up the word body.

Bert is holding the clock next to his **ear.** He can hear the clock ticking.

early Early means too soon.

HOOPER'S
STORE
PARADE TODAY
Bert, did I miss the parade?
No, Ernie, you're **early.** It hasn't started yet.

early Early can also mean near the beginning.

The sun rises **early** in the morning.

earth Earth is the name of the planet on which we live.

Astronaut Grover can see the planet **earth.**

earth Earth is also another word for ground.

The **earth** in Farmer Grover's garden is good for growing carrots.

easy When something is easy, you do not have to work hard to do it.

This is hard.
This is easy.

eat When you eat, you swallow food.

What did you eat for lunch?
I ate a peanut butter sandwich.

egg An egg is a round or oval thing that holds a baby animal until it is ready to be born.

The baby robin is being born.
It is hatching from its **egg.**

Aren't they cute!

eight Eight is a number. Eight is one more than seven.

Oscar has **eight** tin cans in his used-can collection.

eighteen Eighteen is a number. Eighteen is ten plus eight more.

18

Ernie has ten red marbles and eight blue marbles. He has **eighteen** marbles all together.

either Either means one or the other.

Oh, Oscar! You can have **either** the red roses or the stinkweed.
Red roses? Yuk! I'll take the stinkweed.

elbow Your elbow is in the middle of your arm. Your arm bends at the elbow. Look up the word body.

Betty Lou has a bandage on her **elbow.**

elephant An elephant is a big gray animal with a long nose called a trunk.

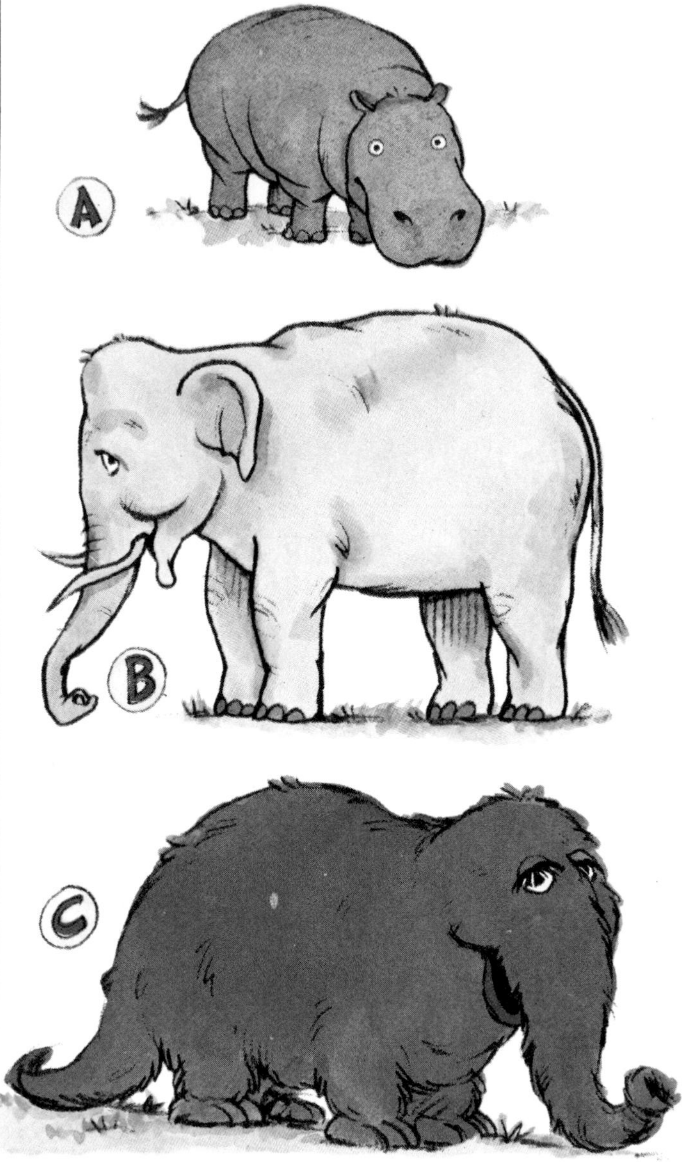
A
B
C

Which of these animals is an **elephant**?
B

elevator An elevator takes people or things up and down in a building.

Grover the **elevator** operator operates an **elevator.**

eleven Eleven is a number. Eleven is ten plus one more.

Bert has ten socks that match and one sock that does not match. He has **eleven** socks all together.

empty When something is empty, there is nothing or no one in it.

The cookie jar is full.
The cookie jar is **empty.**

end The end is the very last part of something.

Big Bird is standing at the **end** of the line.

end When something ends, it is over.

The play will **end** when the curtain comes down.

energy Energy is power to do work. People and machines need energy. Energy for your body comes from food. Energy for machines can come from burning fuel or from the sun.

Farmer Grover uses **energy** from the sun to heat his henhouse.

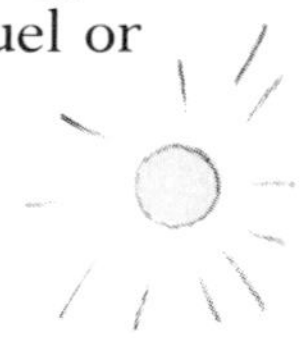

engine An engine is a machine that makes something go.

This tractor will not go unless I turn on the **engine.**

engineer A train engineer is someone who drives a train.

Cookie the train **engineer** is driving the Cookie Express.

engineer An engineer is someone who knows how to build machines or roads or bridges or buildings.

When I grow up, I am going to be an **engineer** and build real bridges.
SHOES

enjoy When you enjoy yourself, you have a good time.

I **enjoy** feeding pigeons.
Here, pigeons!
I **enjoy** counting pigeons. 1, 2, 3, 4, 5... five well-fed pigeons!

enough When you have enough, you have as much as you need.

There are six grouches and six garbage cans. There are **enough** garbage cans for everyone!

The ANNUAL GROUCH PICNIC

PLAZA SESAMO

SUNSET STRIP

PARK AVE.

BOURBON STREET

SESAME STREET

PENNSYLVANIA AVENUE

enter When you enter, you go in.

entrance The entrance is where you go in.

I, Grover, will **enter** through the **entrance.**

MILK BAR

ENTRANCE

MILK BAR

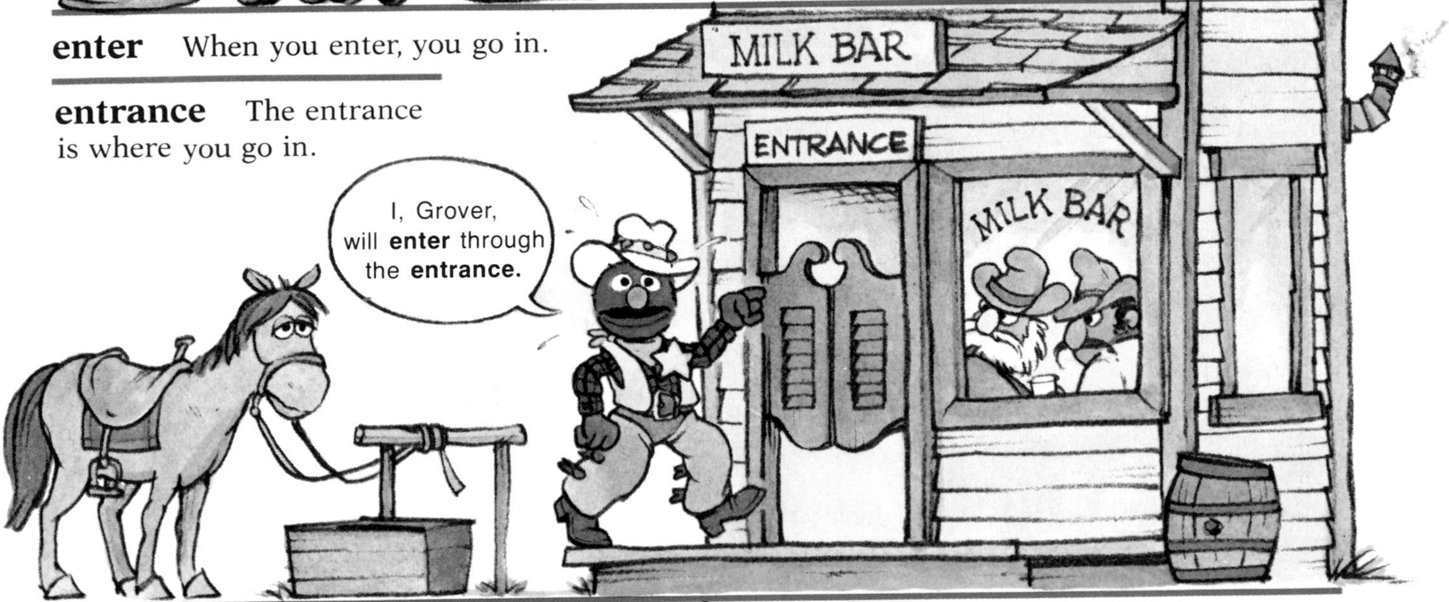

envelope An envelope is a paper container for a letter.

Big Bird has written a letter. He is putting it into an **envelope.**

Mr. Snuffleupagus
Cave South
Central Park, N.Y.

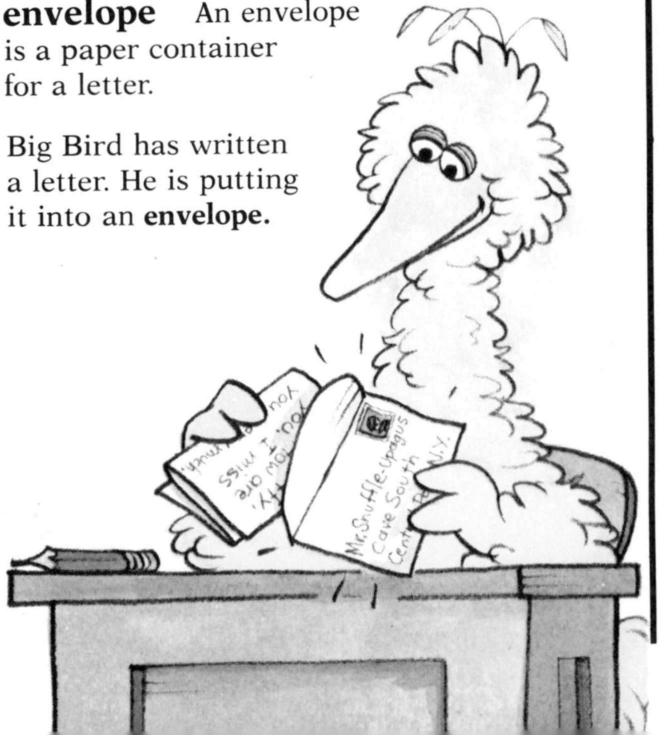

equal When things are equal, they are the same in number or size.

I have three presents.

I have three presents.

1
2
3

1
2
3

The Busby twins have an **equal** number of presents.

equipment Equipment is a set of things you need to do a job.

Biff and Sully are carrying **equipment** to repair the street.

erase When you erase something, you wipe it away.

eraser An eraser is something you use to erase with.

Bert has eight **erasers** in his **eraser** collection.

escalator An escalator is a stairway with moving steps. Escalators can take you up or down.

even When two things or people are even, they are at the same level. They can also be at the same distance from a certain point.

Grover and Betty Lou are riding side by side on the **escalator.** They are **even** with each other.

even Even also means smooth, flat, or level.

Farmer Grover is raking his garden so the ground will be **even.**

ever Ever means at any time or at all times.

MILK BAR
HAW HAW!
HAW HAW!
As our story ends, Marshal Grover is riding into the sunset. Will he **ever** return to Sesame Gulch? Will he **ever** capture Bad Bart? Will he **ever** sit on Fred the right way?

every Every means each one or all.

Every morning the sun comes up in the east.

SESAME GULCH
POP. 8

except Except means leaving out.

Everybody **except** Big Bird is in Big Bird's nest.

Hey, everybody! What about me?

excited You feel excited when you expect something wonderful.

I wonder what is in this package. Oh, I'm so **excited**! Maybe it's a bag of birdseed or a pillow for my nest or…

exercise When you exercise, you make your muscles work.

Exercise is good for you.

Betty Lou and Farley like to **exercise.**

exit The exit is the way out.

The Alphabeats are leaving through the **exit.**

expect When you expect something, you think it will happen.

I, the Amazing Mumford, did not **expect** that!

expensive When something is expensive, it costs a lot of money.

Hey, kid, would you like to buy a letter E?
That's too **expensive.**
E
$8

explain When you explain something, you try to help someone else understand it.

extra When you have an extra amount of something, you have more than you need.

Ernie, please **explain** why you put an **extra** glass on the table. There are only two of us.

eye Your eye is a part of your face. You use your eyes for seeing. Look up the word face.

eyebrow
pupil
eyelid
eyelash

The word exit is an excellent word. Now where is the nearest exit—so I can get out of here?

A B C D E F G H I J K L M N O P Q R S T U V W X Y Z

face Your face is the front part of your head.

Can you name the parts of Bert's **face**?

fact A fact is something that is true.

The tallest living animal is the giraffe.
Is that true?
It's a **fact,** Big Bird.

factory A factory is a building where many people work together to make something.

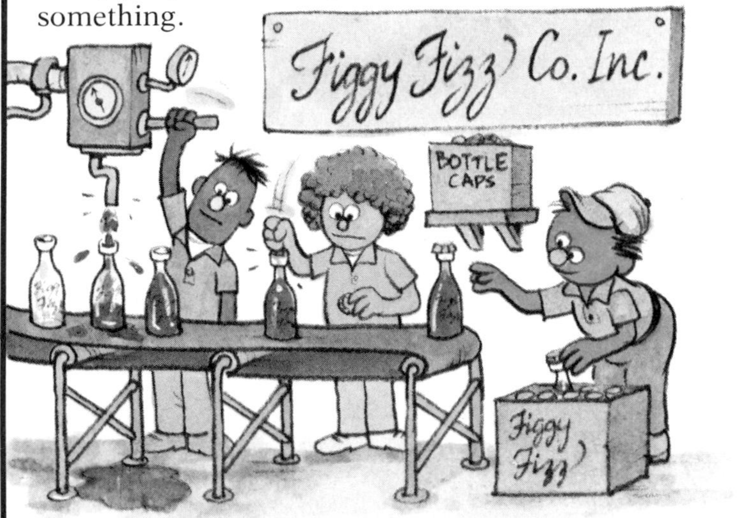

Everyone at the Figgy Fizz **factory** has a different job.

fair When you are fair, you try to treat everyone the same way.

That's not **fair**!
That's **fair**!

fairy A fairy is a make-believe person. Most fairies we read about have wings and magical powers.

There is a picture of a **fairy** in Big Bird's book of **fairy** tales.

FAIRY

A **fairy** tale is a story about **fairies** or other make-believe creatures.

fall Fall is the name of a season. Fall comes after summer.

In the **fall,** the leaves turn beautiful colors.
Fall and autumn are two different names for the same season.

fall When something falls, it drops down.

CTW
SESAME STREET
I love to watch the rain **fall** because I love to count the raindrops.

false When something is false, it is not true.

TRUE OR FALSE!
Hi, everybody! I'm Guy Smiley, everybody's favorite game show host. And here is everybody's favorite game show— TRUE OR **FALSE**?
Me called Big Bird. True or **false**?
Hi! I'm Oscar the Grouch. True or **false**?
I hate this game— true or **false**?

family A family is a group of people who are related.

This is my **family.**
I'm her mother.
I'm her father.
I'm her sister.
I'm her brother.

famous When you are famous, many people know who you are.

Big Bird is a **famous** bird.

fan A fan makes a breeze that helps to keep you cool.

I am cooling off in front of an electric **fan.**
I am cooling off with a paper **fan.**

far When something is far, it is a long distance away.

The moon is very **far** from the earth.

farm A farm is a place where people grow food and raise animals.

farmer A farmer is someone who works on a farm.

Farmer Grover grows corn on his **farm.** He feeds the corn to his pigs.

fast When something moves fast, it moves very quickly.

The hare runs **fast.**
The tortoise walks slowly.

fasten When you fasten something, you make it hold together.

Fasten your seat belt, Prairie Dawn.

fat When something is fat, it is big around.

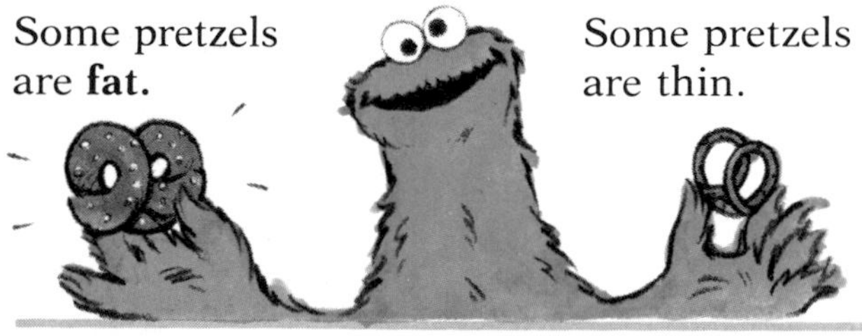

Some pretzels are **fat.**

Some pretzels are thin.

father A father is a man who has a child.

This is my **father.** I call him Dad. My **father** is putting a bandage on my knee. Thanks, Dad.

favorite The one that is your favorite is the one you like the best.

My **favorite** food is birdseed.
My **favorite** food is cabbage.

fear When you fear something, you are afraid of it.

There is nothing to **fear.** The monsters on Sesame Street are friendly.

feather A feather is something that grows on a bird. Feathers help birds to stay warm. They also help them to fly.

Aha! I have found a **feather.** I wonder where it came from.

feed When you feed people or animals, you give them food.

Bert likes to **feed** the pigeons.

feel When you feel something, you touch it. Different things feel different.

I like to **feel** a kitten's fur because it is soft.
A bug **feels** with the **feelers** on top of its head.

feel Feel also means to be or seem a certain way.

LITTLE JERRY AND THE MONOTONES SING ABOUT THEIR FEELINGS
I **feel** happy.
I **feel** sad.
I **feel** hungry.
I **feel** mad.

fence A fence is a kind of wall that is usually outdoors. A fence is usually built to keep things in or out.

I wonder why this **fence** is here.
Oh!

few Few means a small number.

Bert has a **few** bottle caps in the red box. He has many bottle caps in the blue box.

field A field is a large piece of ground where there are no buildings and usually no trees.

Farmer Grover is planting seeds in his **field.**

fifteen Fifteen is a number. Fifteen is ten plus five more.

Cookie the baker made ten round cookies and five square cookies. He made **fifteen** cookies all together.

fight When you fight, you struggle against someone or something.

The job of the fire **fighters** is to **fight** fires.

fill When you fill a container, you put something into it until it will hold no more.

Ernie will **fill** the bathtub with water. When it is **full**, he will take a bath.

find When you find something, you discover it. Sometimes you find things by accident. Sometimes you look for something until you find it.

Egad! I, Sherlock Hemlock, have **found** a mystery. Where is this water coming from?
I will have to keep searching until I **find** the answer.

finger Your finger is a part of your hand. Most people have five fingers on each hand and ten fingers all together. Look up the word body.

How does this monster count to fifteen?
On his **fingers**!

finish When you finish, you come to the end.

Cookie the baker has **finished** baking a cake.

Soon he will **finish** eating the cake.

fire Fire is flame, heat, and light caused by something burning.

fire engine A fire engine is a truck that carries fire fighters and their equipment to a fire.

fire fighter A fire fighter is someone whose job is to put out fires.

The **fire fighters** drove their **fire engine** to the **fire.**

F.D.

first When something is first, it comes before all the others.

Cookie Monster is **first** in line.

COOKIES
FREE COOKIE TO FIRST IN LINE!

fish A fish is an animal that lives in the water. A fish breathes through special openings called gills. Most fish have fins and scales.

Bert is watching the **fish.** The **fish** are watching Bert.

fish To fish means to try to catch a fish.

Herry Monster likes to **fish.**

fit When something fits, it is the right size or shape.

five Five is a number. Five is one more than four.

Herry Monster is eating **five** carrots for lunch.

fix When you fix something, you make it right again.

Betty Lou will **fix** the broken faucet.

flag A flag is a piece of cloth. Most flags have special colors and a special meaning. Every country has its own flag.

Grover is holding the American **flag.**

flat When something is flat, it is not bumpy.

What do monsters eat that is square and green and **flat** as a pancake?
A square green pancake!

flavor The flavor of something is its taste.

I love the **flavor** of chocolate ice cream.
I love the **flavor** of chocolate, too. Heh,heh. I love spinach with chocolate sauce.

float When something floats, it stays on top of the water.

Herry's toy boat can **float** on water.

floor The floor is the part of the room you walk on. Sometimes the floor is covered with a carpet.

What is the first thing a monster puts on when he gets out of bed in the morning?
He puts his feet on the **floor**!

flour Flour is a powder that is made from grain. It is used to make cake, bread, and other things to eat.

Cookie the baker uses **flour** to make cookies.

flower A flower is the part of the plant that has petals. Many flowers have sweet smells and pretty colors.

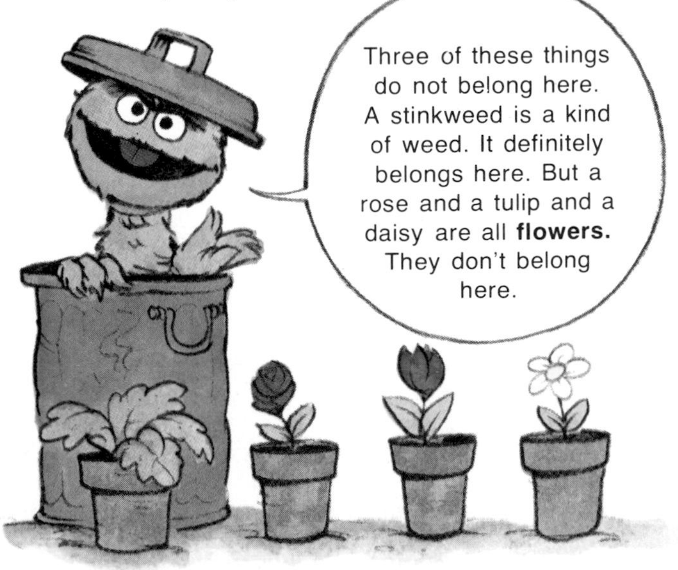
Three of these things do not belong here. A stinkweed is a kind of weed. It definitely belongs here. But a rose and a tulip and a daisy are all **flowers.** They don't belong here.

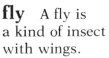

fly A fly is a kind of insect with wings.

Look!
There is another **fly**!
I love to count **flies.**
1, 2, 3, 4, 5...
five fabulous **flies**!
Wonderful!

fly When things fly, they move in the air.

Some birds **fly** and some don't.

fly When you fly something, you make it move in the air.

Grover likes to **fly** his airplane.

Betty Lou likes to **fly** her kite.

fold When you fold something, you bend one part of it over another part.

Bert likes to **fold** laundry.

follow When you follow something, you move along behind it.

Cookie Monster will **follow** anyone with cookies.

food Food is what we eat. All living things need food to help them grow.

Bert is feeding the pigeons some pigeon **food.** Ernie is feeding the plants some plant **food.**

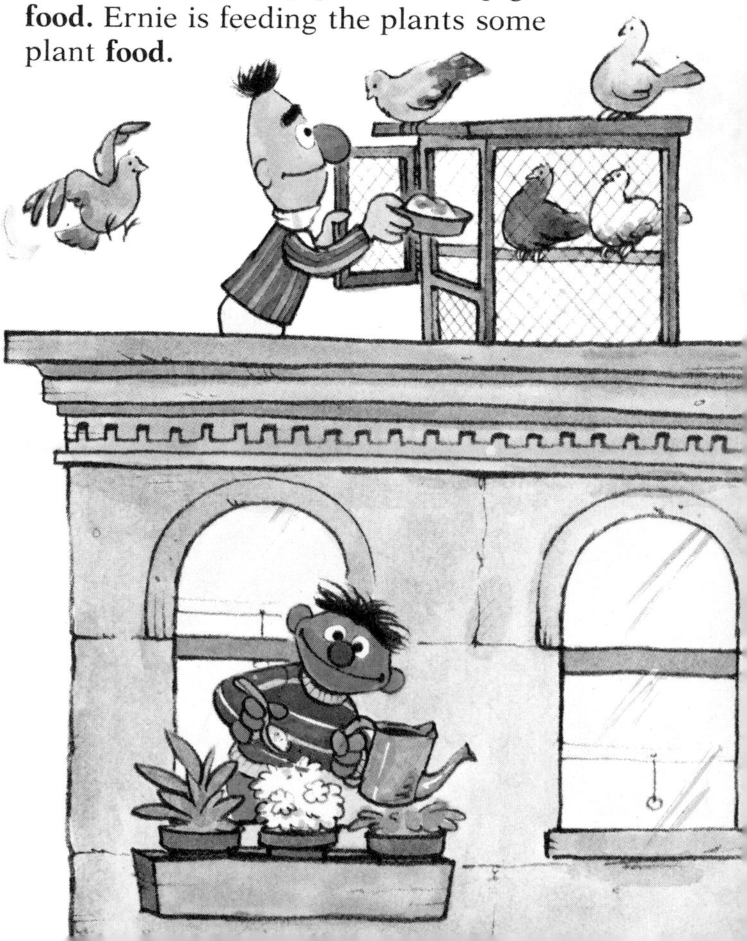

foot A foot is an amount of distance. There are twelve inches in a foot. Look up the word inch.

Bert's paper-clip chain is one **foot** long.

foot Your foot is the part of your body at the end of your leg. Look up the word body.

forehead Your forehead is the part of your face above your eyebrows. Look up the word face.

There is a fly on the Count's **foot** and a fly on his **forehead**.

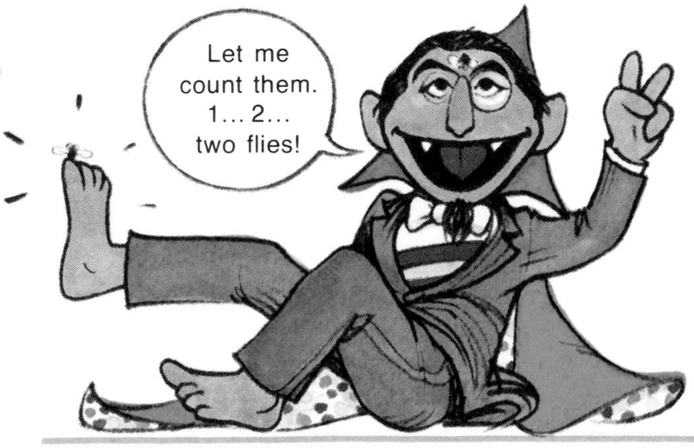

forest A forest is a place where many trees grow.

Prairie Dawn is hiking through the **forest**.

forget When you forget something, you do not remember it.

Bert is going to the store.
What did he **forget**?
He **forgot** his pants.

fork A fork is a tool used to pick things up. Some forks are used to pick up food.

Waiter! This **fork** is dirty.
Bring me a clean **fork**, please.
Here is your clean **fork**, sir.

forward Forward means toward the front or the direction in which your feet are pointing.

The Monster Marching Band is marching **forward**.

four Four is a number. Four is one more than three.

fourteen Fourteen is a number. Fourteen is ten plus four more.

Bert has ten small paper clips and four large paper clips. He has **fourteen** paper clips all together.

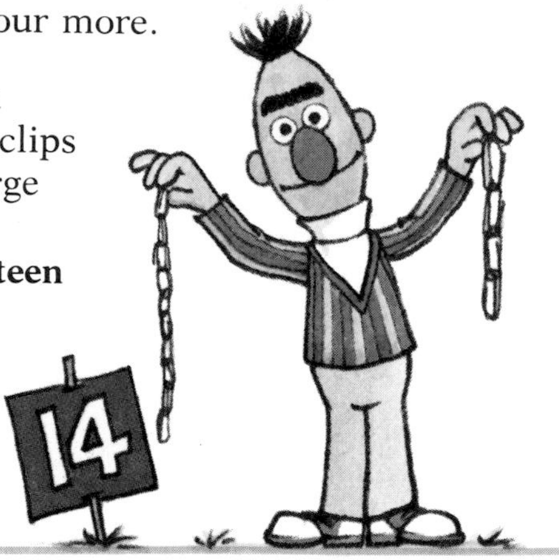

fox A fox is a wild animal with a bushy tail.

The quick brown **fox** jumped over the lazy dog.

free When something is free, it does not cost any money.

Nobody wants my pickle juice even though it is **free.** I don't understand it.
PICKLE JUICE
10¢ 5¢ FREE!

free When you are free, you can move in any direction.

Help! I can't move.
G
Ho-boy! It is good to be **free** again.

freeze When something freezes, it turns to ice.

I had to wait for the pond to **freeze.** Now it is **frozen** and I can ice skate.

friend A friend is someone you like who likes you.

Mr. Snuffle-upagus is my best **friend.**

frighten When you frighten someone, you make that person afraid.

Oscar likes to **frighten** Frazzle.

frog A frog is an animal that lives in or near water. It has webbed feet and strong back legs for jumping. A baby frog is a tadpole.

I can't believe my famous uncle, Kermit the **Frog,** was ever a tadpole.
To Robin Fondly, Kermit

from From means out of.

Cookie Monster got some cookies **from** the cookie jar.

from From also means beginning with.

I know my letters **from** A to Z.
ABCDEFG
HIJKLMN
OPQRSTU
VWXYZ

front The front of something is the part that usually faces forward.

Grover's airplane has a propeller in **front.**

frown When you frown, you look unhappy or angry.

I look so handsome when I **frown.**

fruit A fruit is something that grows on a plant or a tree and holds seeds. Many fruits are sweet and good to eat.

One of these things does not belong in this **fruit** bowl.
An apple, a banana, and an orange are all **fruits.** That blue, furry thing is not a **fruit.**
Cookie Monster, get your paw out of the **fruit** bowl.

fuel Fuel is something that burns to make heat or energy. Wood, coal, gas, and oil are kinds of fuel.

The fire needs more **fuel.** I, Grover, am bringing another piece of wood.

full When something is full, it holds all that it can hold.

Here is a glass of ice-cold Figgy Fizz for my old buddy Bert.
But, Ernie, this glass is almost empty. I want a **full** glass.

Here is a **full** glass, Bert.
But this glass is **full** of marbles. I can't drink marbles.

fun When something is fun, you enjoy it.

You can have a lot of **fun** with marbles.

funny When something is funny, it makes you laugh.

How do you like my Halloween costume, Ernie?
Very **funny,** Bert.

fur Fur is soft, thick hair.

Some animals are covered with **fur.**

Herry Monster's **fur** is blue.

furniture Some of the movable things in a room are called furniture. Tables, chairs, and beds are pieces of furniture.

Hey, Herry, I'm not a piece of **furniture.**

Herry Monster is moving the **furniture.**

Of all the F words, my favorite is frown. That's a fact.

A B C D E F **G** H I J K L M N O P Q R S T U V W X Y Z

game A game is something that you play in a special way.

HIDE and SEEK!
Hi, folks! This is Guy Smiley, everybody's favorite **game** show host, bringing you everybody's favorite **game**—HIDE AND SEEK!
Four friends from Sesame Street are hiding. If you want to play this **game,** you must find them.

garage A garage is a special place used to park cars.

The Count is driving his bat car into the **garage.**

garage A garage is also a building where mechanics repair cars.

Prairie Dawn
is a **garage** mechanic.
She works at the Dawn-to-Dusk **Garage.**

garbage Garbage is leftover food that is thrown away.

The **garbage** collector is collecting the **garbage.** He empties the **garbage** cans into the **garbage** truck.

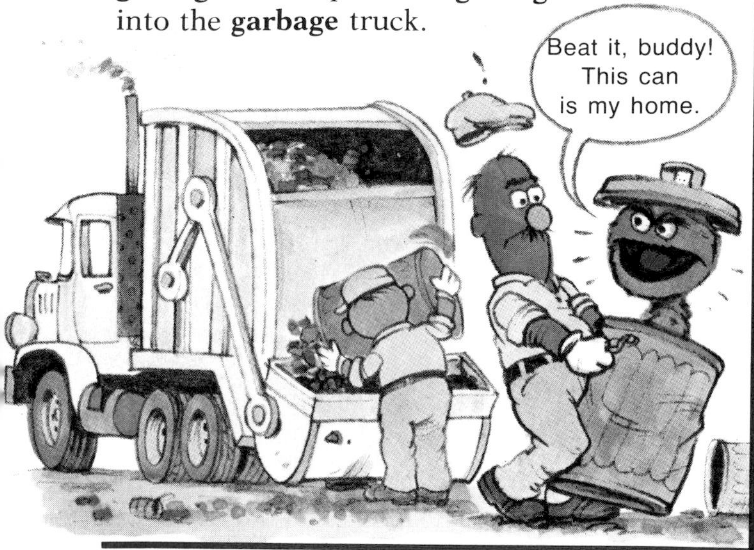

Beat it, buddy! This can is my home.

garden A garden is a place where someone has planted flowers or vegetables.

Farmer Grover planted six different kinds of vegetables in his **garden.**

gate A gate is a door in a fence or wall.

Herry Monster is opening the **gate.**

get When you get something, you receive it.

Oscar **gets** his mud from the Mudman.

giant Giant means very big.

Big Bird found a **giant** toothbrush. It belongs to Snuffle-upagus.

gift A gift is a present.

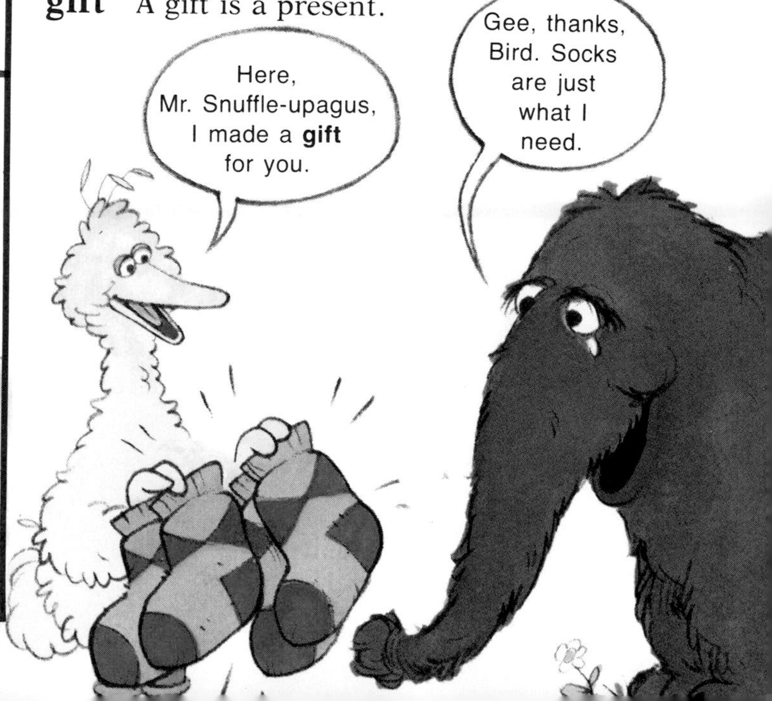

Here, Mr. Snuffle-upagus, I made a **gift** for you.
Gee, thanks, Bird. Socks are just what I need.

giraffe A giraffe is the tallest animal in the world. It has a very long neck and eats leaves.

give When you give something to someone, you hand it to that person.

Grover bought some flowers to **give** to his mother.

Thank you, Grover. These are the most beautiful flowers you ever **gave** me.

glad When you are glad, you are happy.

I'm **glad** you're my friend, Bird.

girl A girl is a child who will grow up to be a woman.

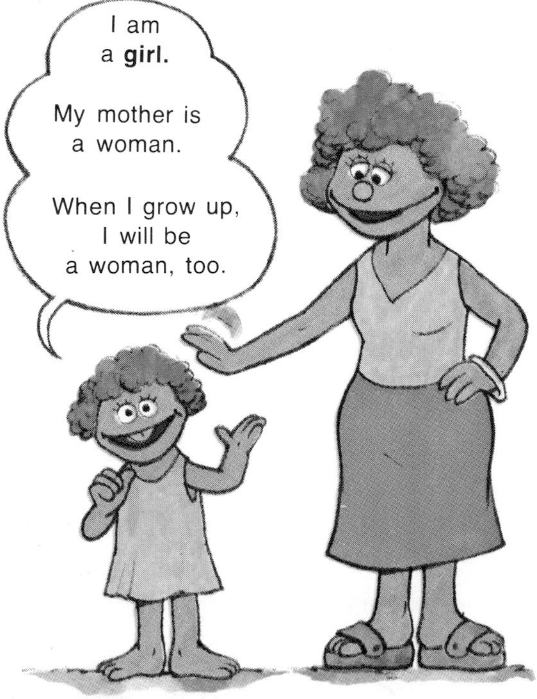

I am a **girl.**
My mother is a woman.
When I grow up, I will be a woman, too.

glass Glass is hard and smooth and breakable. You can see through most glass.

Three of these things belong together. One of these things is not the same.

A mirror, a window, and a **glass** slipper are all made out of **glass.** A cowgirl boot is made out of leather. The boot does not belong.

glasses Glasses help people who do not see well to see better.

Mr. Chatterly wears **glasses** to help him see.

glove A glove is a cover for your hand. It helps protect your hand and keeps it warm. Most gloves have places for five fingers.

Cookie the baker wears rubber **gloves** when he washes the dishes.

glue Glue is wet and sticky and is used to join things together.

Ernie is using **glue** to put his model airplane together.

go When you go, you move from one place to another.

Here I **go**! Good-by, everybod-ee!
Where did he **go**?
He **went** that way.
Now he is **gone.**

goat A goat is an animal with hoofs and horns.

Farmer Grover's **goats** are in the vegetable garden.

I am a baby **goat.** I am a kid.
I am the kid's mother. I am a nanny **goat.**
I am the kid's father. I am a billy **goat.**

gold Gold is a heavy yellow metal. Coins and jewelry are often made of gold.

At last I have found the buried treasure! Now I can count it. One piece of **gold,** two pieces of **gold,** three pieces of **gold** ...

gone When something is gone, it is no longer there.

Zounds! The cookies are **gone**!
The plate is **gone**!
Even the table is **gone**!

good Something that is good is done well.

That is a **good** trick, Betty Lou.

good When you are happy or healthy, you feel good.

Betty Lou has lots of energy. She feels **good.**

good A good person is kind and thinks of other people.

Would you like to share my sandwich, Sully?

Biff is a **good** friend.

goose A goose is a large bird. Some geese live on farms. Some geese are wild.

I am a baby **goose.** I am a gosling.
I am the gosling's mother. I am a **goose.**
I am the gosling's father. I am a gander.

The **geese** are swimming in the lake.

grab When you grab something, you take hold of it suddenly.

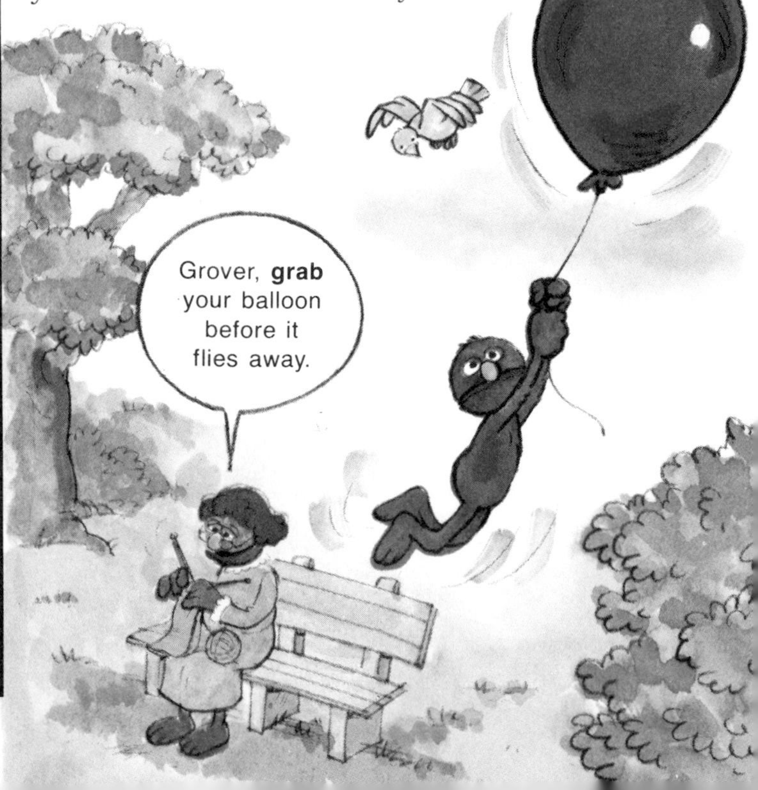
Grover, **grab** your balloon before it flies away.

grain A grain is a tiny piece of something.

When I am at the beach, I can count each **grain** of sand.

grain Grain is also the food that cereal and flour are made from.

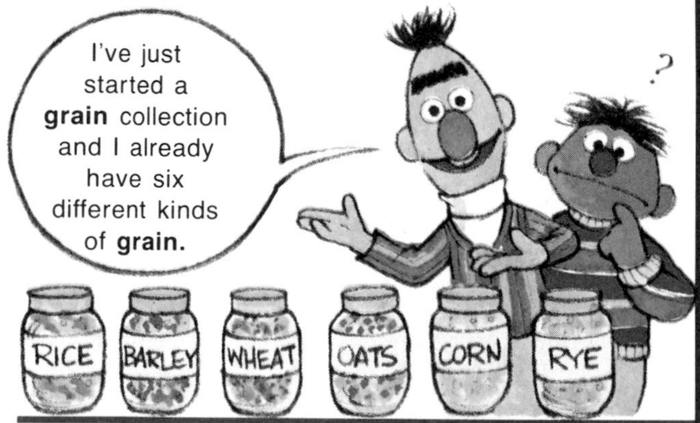
I've just started a **grain** collection and I already have six different kinds of **grain.**
?
RICE
BARLEY
WHEAT
OATS
CORN
RYE

grandparents Your grandparents are the parents of your father or mother.

GRANDFATHER
GRANDMOTHER
MOTHER
FATHER
GRANDMOTHER
GRANDFATHER

grape A grape is a small, round fruit that grows in bunches on vines.

Betty Lou is picking **grapes.**

grass Grass is a plant that covers the ground. Some grass is short and green. Some is tall and golden.

Farmer Grover's cows are eating the **grass** in the pasture.

great When something is great, it is bigger or better than usual.

Gee, Rodeo Rosie, that's a **great** trick!

grocery store A grocery store is a place where you can buy food and supplies which are called groceries. The person who sells groceries is the grocer.

Bert is buying **groceries** from the **grocer** at the **grocery store.**

grouch A grouch is someone who complains a lot.

What is **grouchier** than a **grouch**?
Two **grouches**!

ground The ground is the solid top part of the earth.

Grover's airplane is on the **ground.**

group A group is a collection of people or things.

A **group** of monsters is walking down the street.

grow When something grows, it becomes bigger.

Jack's beanstalk began to **grow,** and it kept on **growing** and **growing** and **growing.**

grow When you grow something, you put a seed or a plant in dirt and take care of it so that it will get bigger.

I like to **grow** many different kinds of plants in my backyard.

guard A guard is someone who protects people or things.

The crossing **guard** helps the children to cross the street.

The life**guard** is **guarding** the swimmers.

guess When you guess, you think of an answer without knowing for sure.

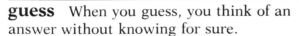

guest A guest is someone who comes to visit.

Guess who will not be a **guest** for dinner again?

guitar A guitar is a musical instrument with strings.

Cowboy Ernie is strumming his **guitar.**

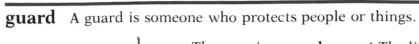

? ?
Where are all the great words that begin with G—words like grimy, grubby, and grumpy?

A B C D E F G **H** I J K L M N O P Q R S T U V W X Y Z

hair Hair grows on the top of your head and on other parts of your body. Look up the word body.

My **hair** is long and straight.
My **hair** is short and curly.
Animal **hair** is sometimes called fur...
...or wool.

half A half is one of two equal parts. The two parts together make a whole thing.

Zounds! **Half** of the pie is missing!

hammer A hammer is a tool for hitting nails and other things.

Prairie Dawn is building a tree house. She is using a **hammer** to pound a nail into the wood.

hand Your hand is the part of your body at the end of your arm. Look up the word body.

Prairie Dawn is holding a **hammer** in her **hand**.

handle The handle of something is the part that you hold on to.

Biff's lunchbox has a **handle.**

Sully's hammer has a **handle.**

handsome When something is handsome, it is nice to look at.

I think my snuffle is very **handsome.**

hang To hang means to be attached to something above.

Betty Lou can **hang** by her knees.

When you hang on, you hold tightly.

Hang on, Tessie!

happen When something happens, it takes place.

Why do these things always **happen** to me?

happy When you are happy, you feel good about things.

The Count is **happy.**

four bats.

I love to count bats.

hard When something is hard, you cannot easily change its shape. When something feels hard, it does not feel soft.

Ouch! This rock is **hard.**
A sheep's wool is soft.

hard When something is hard to do, it takes extra work or special skill. It is not easy to do.

It's easy to make cookies.
But it's **hard** to wait while they bake.

hat A hat is something that you wear on your head.

Hi! I'm Guy Smiley, here to play— THE **HAT** GAME! Find the **hat** that belongs to each of our guests!
The HAT GAME

hatch When baby animals hatch, they come out of eggs.

I wonder when they will **hatch.**
Oh! They are **hatching.**
Oh! They have **hatched** and they are so cute.
I **have** some new chicks. They **have** cute little yellow feathers.

Farmer Grover **had** six eggs. Now he **has** six chicks.

have When you have something, it belongs to you.

have Have also means to be holding or keeping something for someone else.

I think I **have** your scarf, Big Bird.
I think I **have** yours, Little Bird.

hay Hay is a kind of grass that has been cut and dried. Cows and horses eat hay.

Farley dropped his sewing needle in a pile of **hay.**

he He is another way to say man or boy or male animal.

Sherlock Hemlock is looking for a needle in a haystack. Do you think that **he** will find it?

head Your head is the part of your body above your neck. Look up the word body.

Bert has a pot on his **head.**

healthy When you are healthy, you feel well and your body works the way it should.

I do exercises to stay **healthy.**

hear You use your ears to hear sounds.

Super Grover has super **hearing.**

I, Super Grover, can **hear** the sound of a cookie jar being opened in the next room.
COOKIES

heart Your heart is inside your chest. It pumps blood to all parts of your body. Look up the word blood.

The doctor is listening to Betty Lou's **heart.** She can hear it with her stethoscope.

A **heart** is also a special shape.

heavy Something that is heavy is harder to lift than something that is light.

Say, Ernie, why is it that I am carrying the piano and you are carrying the piano stool?

Gee, Bert. I thought the piano *and* the piano stool would be too **heavy** for you.

heel Your heel is the back part of your foot. Look up the word body.

height The height of something is how tall or high it is.

The Count is measuring Big Bird's **height** from his **heel** to the top of his head.

242... 243...244... two hundred and forty-four centimeters! That is ninety-six inches.

8 ft.

heel

helicopter A helicopter is a flying machine with a large propeller on top. Helicopters can fly in any direction.

Granny Fanny Nesselrode is flying in her **helicopter.** She can see the tops of the buildings.

Gray 6

hello Hello is something you usually say when you greet someone.

What do you say when you meet a two-headed monster?

? ?

Hello. Hello.

What's new?

How are you?

helmet A helmet is a hard hat that is used to protect the head.

Super Grover wears a **helmet.**

help When you help someone, you find ways to make things easier or nicer for that person.

Super Grover likes to **help.**

The ADVENTURES of SUPER GROVER
When I put on my **helmet,** I change into brave and fearless... SUPER GROVER! Now I must find someone who needs my **help.**

hen A hen is a female chicken. Some other female birds are also called hens.

Super Grover saw a **hen.**

This is boring sitting here all day keeping these eggs warm. I could use some **help.**

her Her is another way to say woman or girl or female animal. It can also mean belonging to a woman, a girl, or a female animal.

The hen was tired of sitting on **her** eggs. Super Grover wanted to help **her.**

There is someone who needs my **help.** Down, down, and away!
HELP! HELP!

here Here means in this place.

Here is a picture of Super Grover and the hen.

Get out of **here,** you...you... you furry blue thing!
Oh, do not thank me! I am happy to **help.** We super**heroes** live to serve.

hero A hero is someone who is brave and fearless and very helpful.

Super Grover thinks he is a **hero.**

THE END

hide When you hide, you stay where no one can see you. When you hide something, you put it where no one can find it.

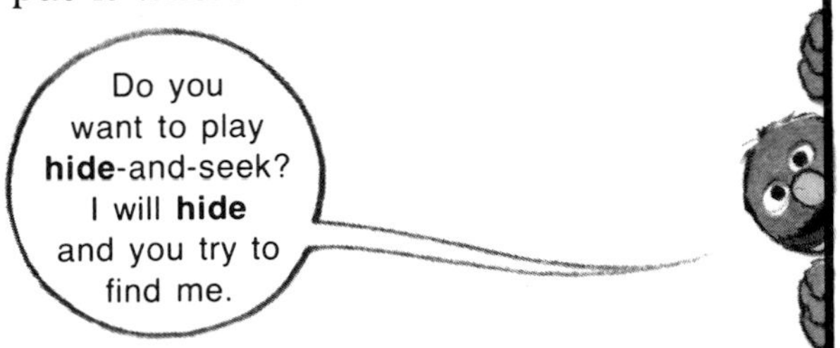

Do you want to play **hide**-and-seek? I will **hide** and you try to find me.

high Something that is high is farther up than something that is low.

I can reach the **high** shelf.
BIRD SEED
I can reach the low shelf.
BIRD SEED

hill A hill is a small mountain.

Prairie Dawn is climbing up the **hill.**

him Him is another way to say man or boy or male animal.

Herry Monster lost his doll. Betty Lou returned it to **him.**

hip Your hips are on both sides of your body below your waist. Look up the word body.

Prairie Dawn is dancing with her hands on her **hips.**

hippopotamus A hippopotamus is a big animal with a large head, short legs, and thick skin. It lives in a river or a lake.

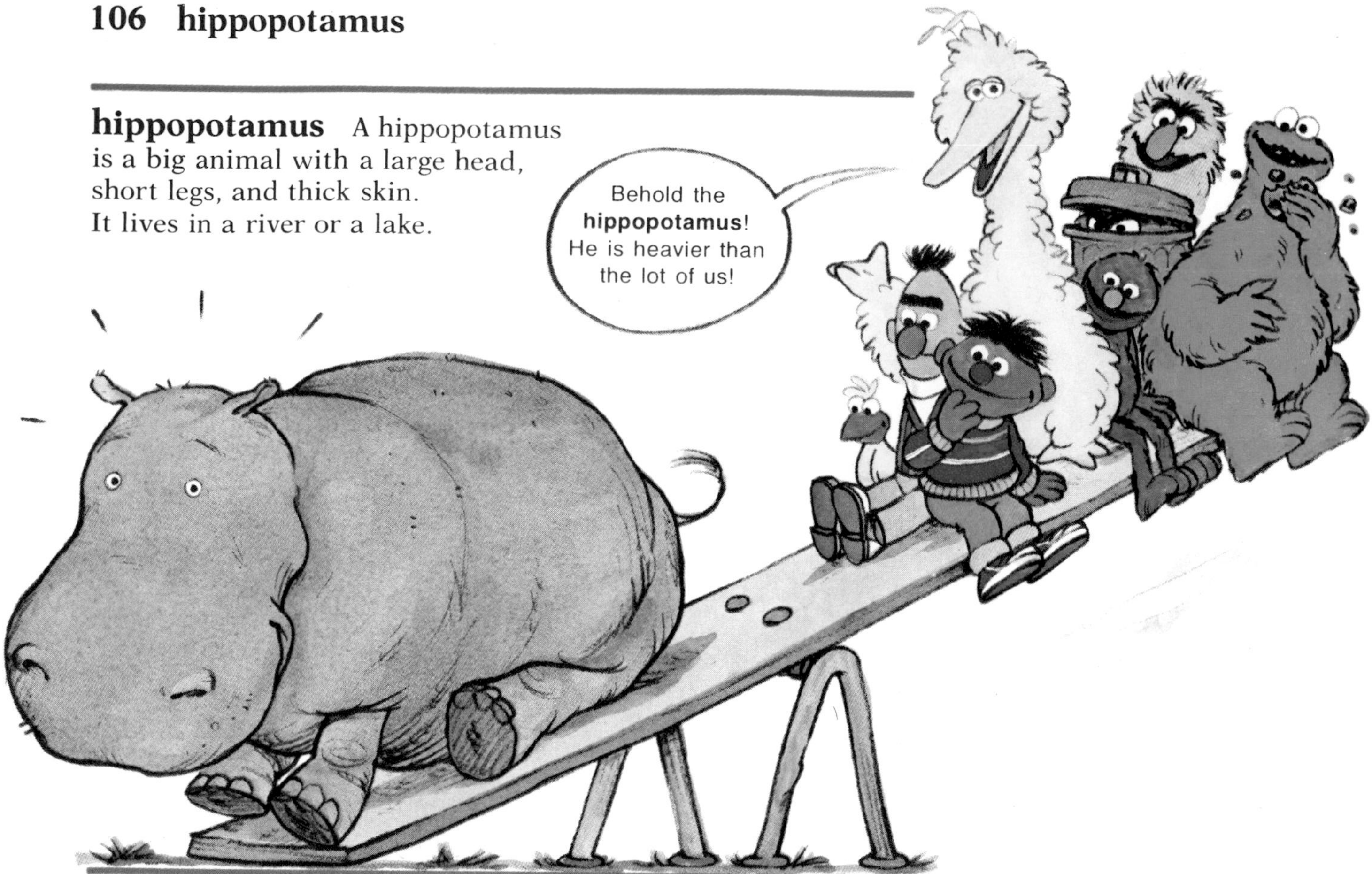

Behold the **hippopotamus**! He is heavier than the lot of us!

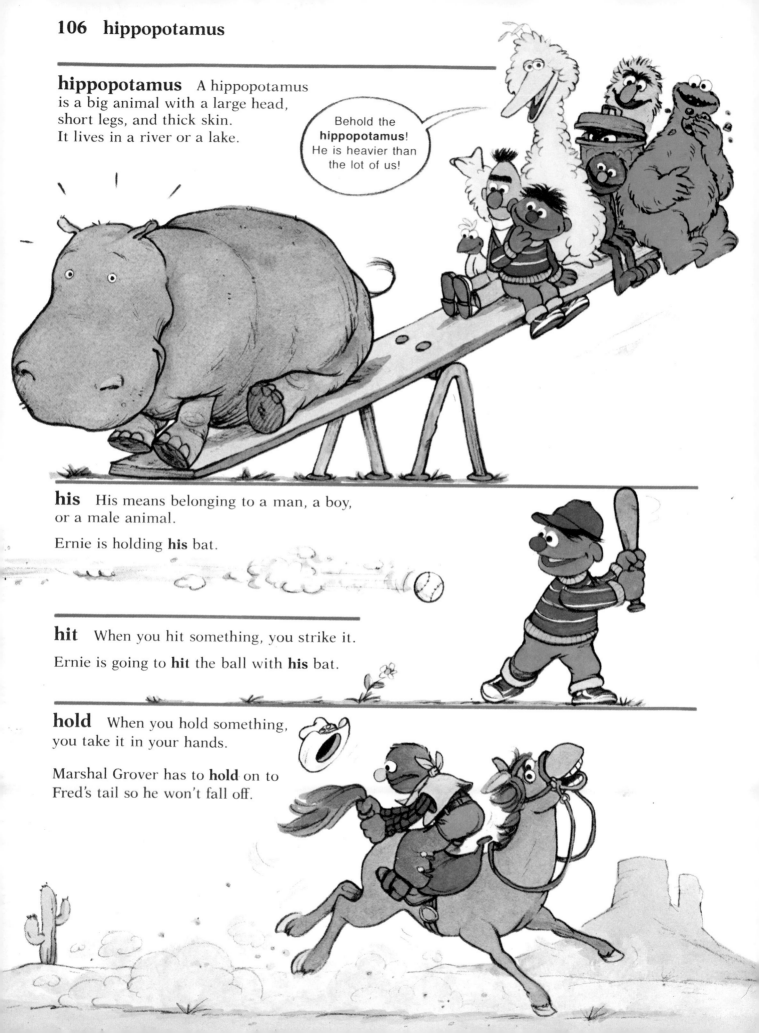

his His means belonging to a man, a boy, or a male animal.

Ernie is holding **his** bat.

hit When you hit something, you strike it.

Ernie is going to **hit** the ball with **his** bat.

hold When you hold something, you take it in your hands.

Marshal Grover has to **hold** on to Fred's tail so he won't fall off.

hold Hold also means to keep something in place. Containers can hold many different things.

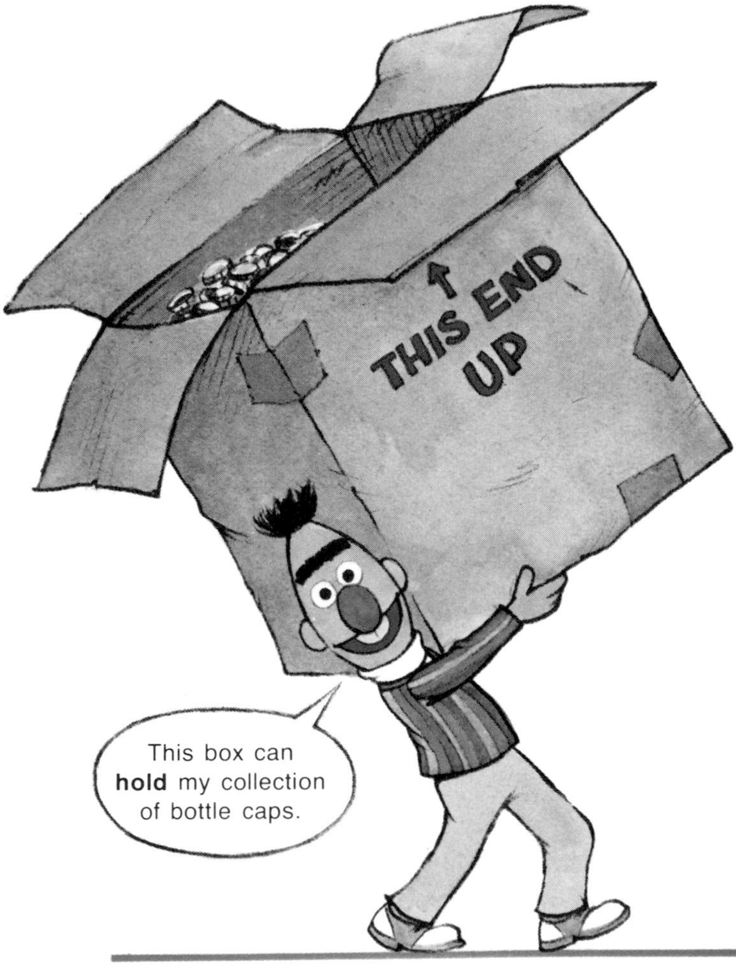

THIS END UP
This box can **hold** my collection of bottle caps.

hole A hole is an opening in something.

Super Grover has a **hole** in his cape.

holiday A holiday is a special day in the year when people celebrate something. On some holidays people do not work or go to school.

The Fourth of July is a **holiday.** On the Fourth of July we celebrate the birthday of the United States.

home Your home is the place where you live.

Ernie and Bert's **home** is in an apartment house.

Big Bird's **home** is a nest.

honey Honey is a sweet syrup made by bees.

The queen is in the parlor
eating bread and **honey.**

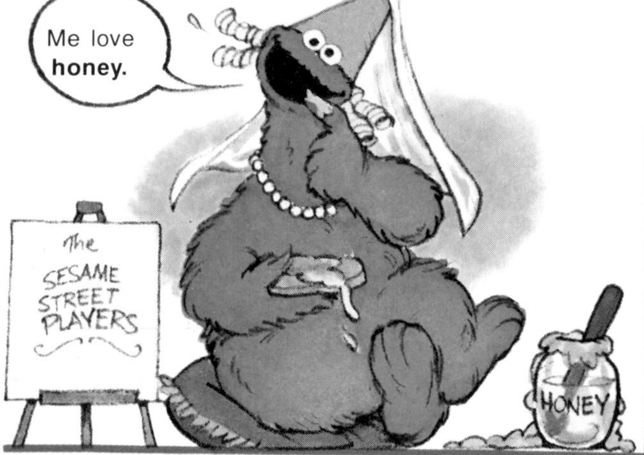
Me love **honey.**
The SESAME STREET PLAYERS
HONEY

hook A hook is used to hold things, catch things, or fasten things. A hook is bent at one end.

Can you find three kinds of **hooks**
in this picture?

hop When you hop, you jump up and down.

Grover loves to **hop.**
He is playing **hop**scotch.

Do you see how I am **hopping** from square number one to square number two?
1
2
3
4
5
6
7
HOME

horn A horn is a musical instrument that you blow into.

horn A horn is also something that makes a loud noise to warn people.

horn The horns on the heads of some animals are made of bone or hair and are used for protection.

I, the Amazing Mumford, will now pull from this perfectly empty hat three different things with the same name.
A LA PEANUT BUTTER SANDWICHES!

Now where is that other kind of **horn**?
It's right behind you, Mumphie!

horse A horse is an animal with four long legs, a mane, and a tail. People can ride on horses.

I am a baby **horse.** I am a foal.
I am the foal's mother. I am a mare.
Whoa, Fred!
I am the foal's father. I am a stallion.

Some **horses** can run very fast.

hospital A hospital is a building where people go when they need special help from doctors.

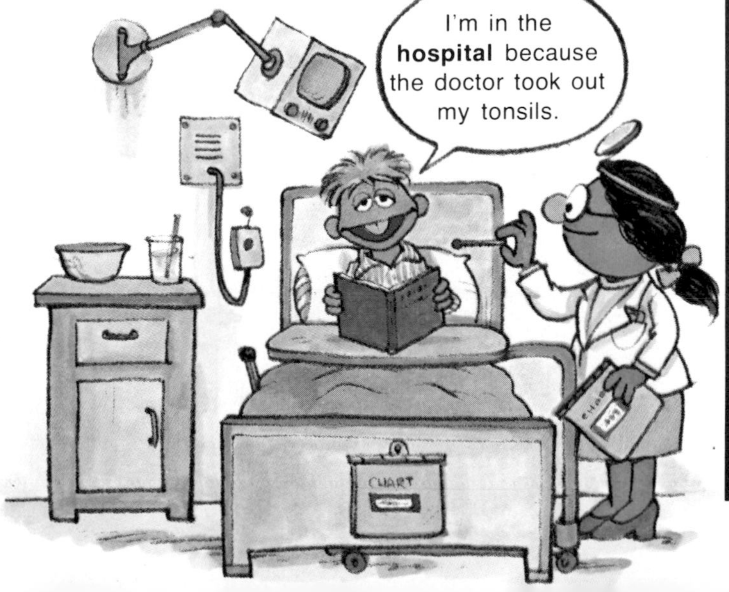
I'm in the **hospital** because the doctor took out my tonsils.
CHART

hot When something is hot, it is very, very warm.

Oh! This porridge is **hot**!
What a **hot** day!
The SESAME STREET PLAYERS
GOLDILOCKS AND THE 3 BEARS

hotel A hotel is a building where people pay money to sleep and eat when they are away from home.

Granny Fanny Nesselrode is going to stay at the Sesame Gulch **Hotel.**

SGH
SESAME GULCH HOTEL
CABLE T.V.

hour An hour is an amount of time. An hour is sixty minutes long.

Hey, Bert. It takes one **hour** for my pet fish to swim a hundred laps.
Are you through with the bathtub, Ernie?

house A house is a building to live in. Some houses are big enough for only one family. Apartment houses are big enough for many families.

I live in a **house.**
I live in an apartment **house.**

I live in a bird**house.**

how How means in what way or in this way.

Can you tell me **how** to get to Sesame Street?
Sure. Follow that bird.

hug When you hug someone, you put your arms around that person.

huge When something is huge, it is very, very big.

Snuffle-upagus is too **huge** to **hug.**

hundred One hundred is a number. One hundred is one more than ninety-nine.

There are one **hundred** cents in a dollar.

97...98... 99...100... one **hundred** cents! Wonderful!

hungry When you feel hungry, you want to eat.

Biff and Sully are **hungry.** They are having lunch.

hunt When you hunt for something, you look for it.

hurry When you hurry, you move faster than usual.

Sherlock, I lost Rubber Duckie.
Have no fear. I, Sherlock Hemlock, the world's greatest detective, will **hunt** for it.
Please **hurry**, Sherlock. I can't take my bath without Rubber Duckie.

hurt When you hurt, you feel pain.

Frazzle bumped his foot. His foot **hurts.**

husband A husband is a man who is married.

I am married to him. He's my **husband.**
I am married to her. She's my wife.

This dictionary has left out a good H word— heap!
Some of my favorite heaps are junk heaps, garbage heaps, and rubbish heaps.

A B C D E F G H I J K L M N O P Q R S T U V W X Y Z

I I is a word you use when you are talking or thinking about yourself.

ice Ice is frozen water.

Herry Monster is skating on the **ice.**

I like to skate on the **ice.**
I think he should be more careful.
I think this **ice** is cold.

ice cream Ice cream is a sweet, frozen food made with cream and sugar.

idea An idea is a thought in someone's mind.

ICE CREAM
Now, what shall I do with this extra **ice cream** cone?
I have a good **idea.**

if If means supposing that.

imagination You use your imagination to think of things that are not right in front of you or things that are not real.

If Mr. Snuffle-upagus had wings, he would be a snuffle-bird.

Big Bird has a good **imagination.**

immediately Immediately means right now.

Operator? Get me the Mudman **immediately**! I'm out of mud.

important When something is important, it matters very much to someone.

Clues are **important.**

impossible When something is impossible, it cannot be done.

I would like a peanut butter sandwich without any bread.
That is **impossible,** sir! You cannot make a sandwich without bread.
MENU

in In means within or surrounded by. In means not out.

Little Bird is **in** his nest.

Cookie Monster has his hand **in** the cookie jar.

inch An inch is an amount of distance. There are twelve inches in a foot.

The six of us together are an **inch** long.
1 in.

insect An insect is a tiny animal with six legs. Some insects have wings. Some do not.

Dragonfly
My favorite **insect** is the ladybug.

inside Inside means within.

instead Instead means in place of.

I, the Amazing Mumford, will now pull from this perfectly empty hat a beautiful silk scarf.
A LA PEANUT BUTTER SANDWICHES!
?
That's strange! I pulled out a rabbit **instead** of a scarf.

interesting When something is interesting, it holds your attention.

That's an **interesting** rock, Bert.
Yes, it has many beautiful colors in it, Ernie.
Gee, Bert. I just thought it was **interesting** because there's a great big spider crawling on it.

into When you go into something, you enter it.

Farmer Grover is driving his tractor **into** the barn.

invisible When something is invisible, you cannot see it.

Air is all around you, but it is **invisible.**

invite When you invite someone, you ask that person to come for a visit or to do something with you.

invitation An invitation is used to ask someone to a party or a special occasion.

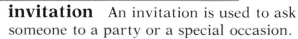

iron An iron is a tool used to smooth the wrinkles out of clothes. An iron must be heated before it can be used.

Bert is **ironing** his pigeon costume with an **iron.**

is Grover's favorite story **is** about Super Grover.

island An island is a piece of land that is surrounded by water.

Once upon a time Super Grover was flying over a small **island.**

it It is a word you use when you are talking or thinking about a thing.

Look at all that poison ivy. I will be careful not to step in **it.**
Don't touch **it**! Don't walk in **it**! Don't pick **it**! Don't...

...land in **it**!
Poison ivy will give you an **itch.**

THE END

itch An itch is a feeling that makes you want to scratch your skin.

Super Grover has an **itch.**

A B C D E F G H I J K L M N O P Q R S T U V W X Y Z

jacket A jacket is a short coat.

Hey, Ernie. How do you like my nifty new **jacket**?
PIGEON LOVERS' CLUB

jar A jar is a kind of container that is usually made of glass. It has a large opening at the top.

Oscar keeps his pickles in a **jar.**

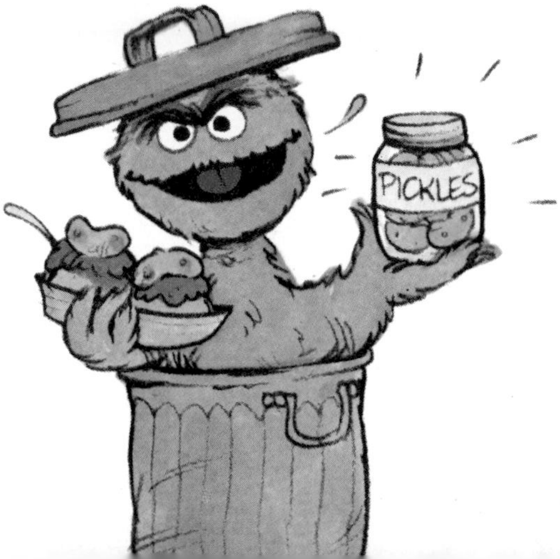
PICKLES

job A job is work that you do. Most people are paid money for doing their jobs.

Hi! My name is Don Music, and my **job** is writing songs.

I'm the Mudman, and my **job** is delivering mud. Oscar is my best customer.
MUD

join When you join things, you put them together.

Let's all **join** hands and make a circle.

join When you join a group, you become part of it.

If you **join** the Pigeon Lovers' Club, you can wear one of these nifty jackets.
The PIGEON LOVERS' CLUB
PLC
PLC
PLC
PLC

joke A joke is something you say or do that is funny.

Hey, Ernie. Did you take a bath this morning?
No, Bert. Is there one missing? Hee hee!

That's a very funny **joke,** Ernie! Now clean up your mess!

juice Juice is the liquid that comes out of a fruit or vegetable.

Betty Lou is thirsty.
She is drinking
a glass of orange **juice.**

glug
glug

jump When you jump, both of your feet leave the ground at the same time.

Who can **jump** higher than a house — Grover or Herry Monster?
Both of us can! Houses can't **jump.**

jungle A jungle is a place full of trees and vines. A jungle is usually warm and damp.

Do you know why I love the **jungle**? The **jungle** is full of interesting animals to count. 1, 2, 3, 4...four interesting animals!

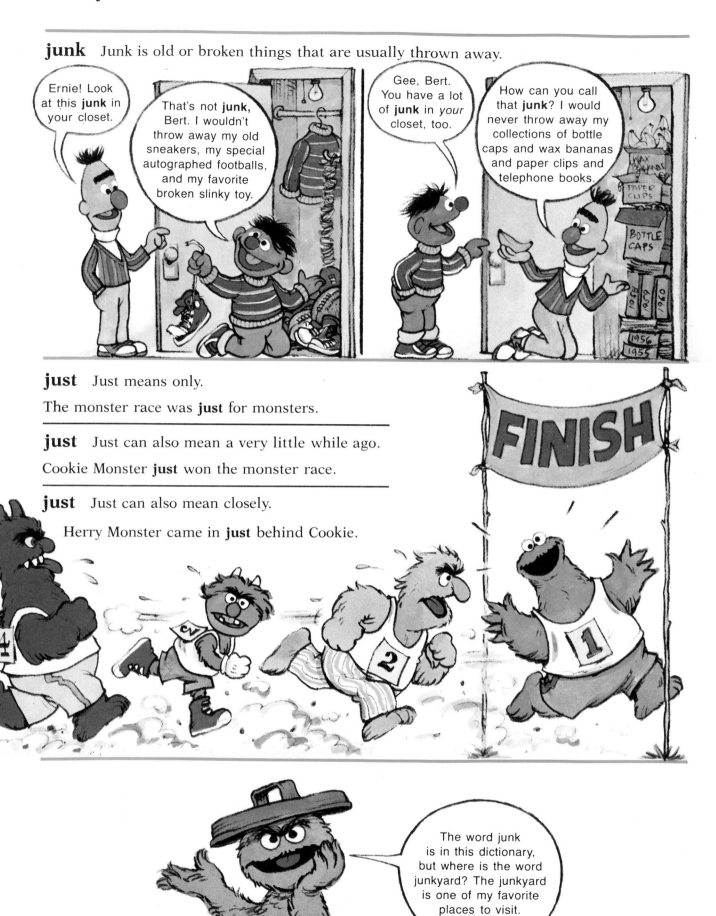

junk Junk is old or broken things that are usually thrown away.

junk Junk is old or broken things that are usually thrown away.

Ernie! Look at this **junk** in your closet.

That's not **junk**, Bert. I wouldn't throw away my old sneakers, my special autographed footballs, and my favorite broken slinky toy.

Gee, Bert. You have a lot of **junk** in *your* closet, too.

How can you call that **junk**? I would never throw away my collections of bottle caps and wax bananas and paper clips and telephone books.

just Just means only.

The monster race was **just** for monsters.

just Just can also mean a very little while ago.

Cookie Monster **just** won the monster race.

just Just can also mean closely.

Herry Monster came in **just** behind Cookie.

The word junk is in this dictionary, but where is the word junkyard? The junkyard is one of my favorite places to visit.

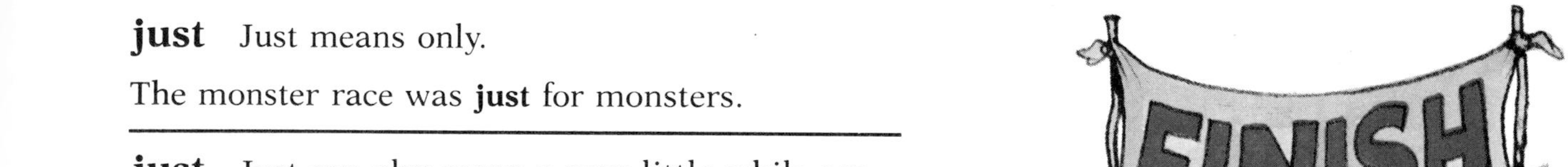

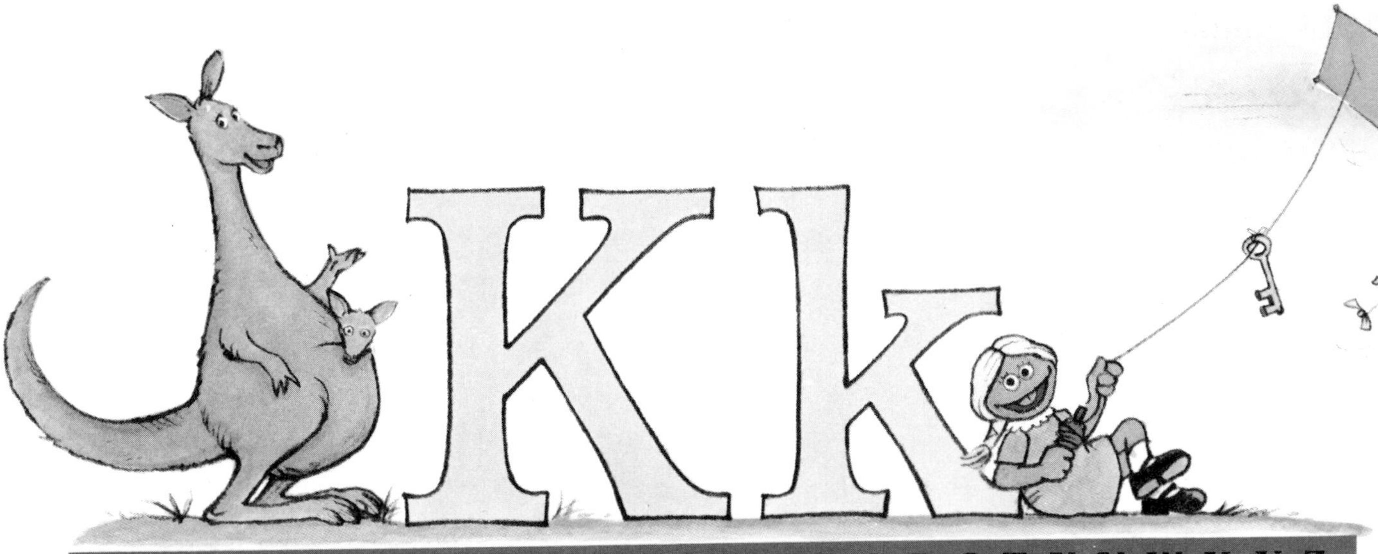

A B C D E F G H I J **K** L M N O P Q R S T U V W X Y Z

kangaroo A kangaroo is an animal that has strong back legs for jumping. A mother kangaroo carries her baby in a pouch.

I am a baby **kangaroo.** I am a joey.
We are the joey's mother and father. We are **kangaroos.**

keep When you keep something, you have it. Sometimes you hold it and sometimes you put it in a special place.

Ernie! Why are all of your marbles in the cookie jar?
That's where I **keep** my marble collection.
COOKIES
Then where are you **keeping** the cookies I made this morning?
I'm **keeping** them in a special place.
COOKIES
What special place?
My stomach!
COOKIES

keep When you keep doing something, you go on doing it.

As long as the sheep **keep** jumping, I will **keep** counting them. 108, 109, 110...

key A key is something that is used to open a lock.

keyhole A keyhole is an opening for a key.

The castle door was locked. Prince Charming put the **key** into the **keyhole.**

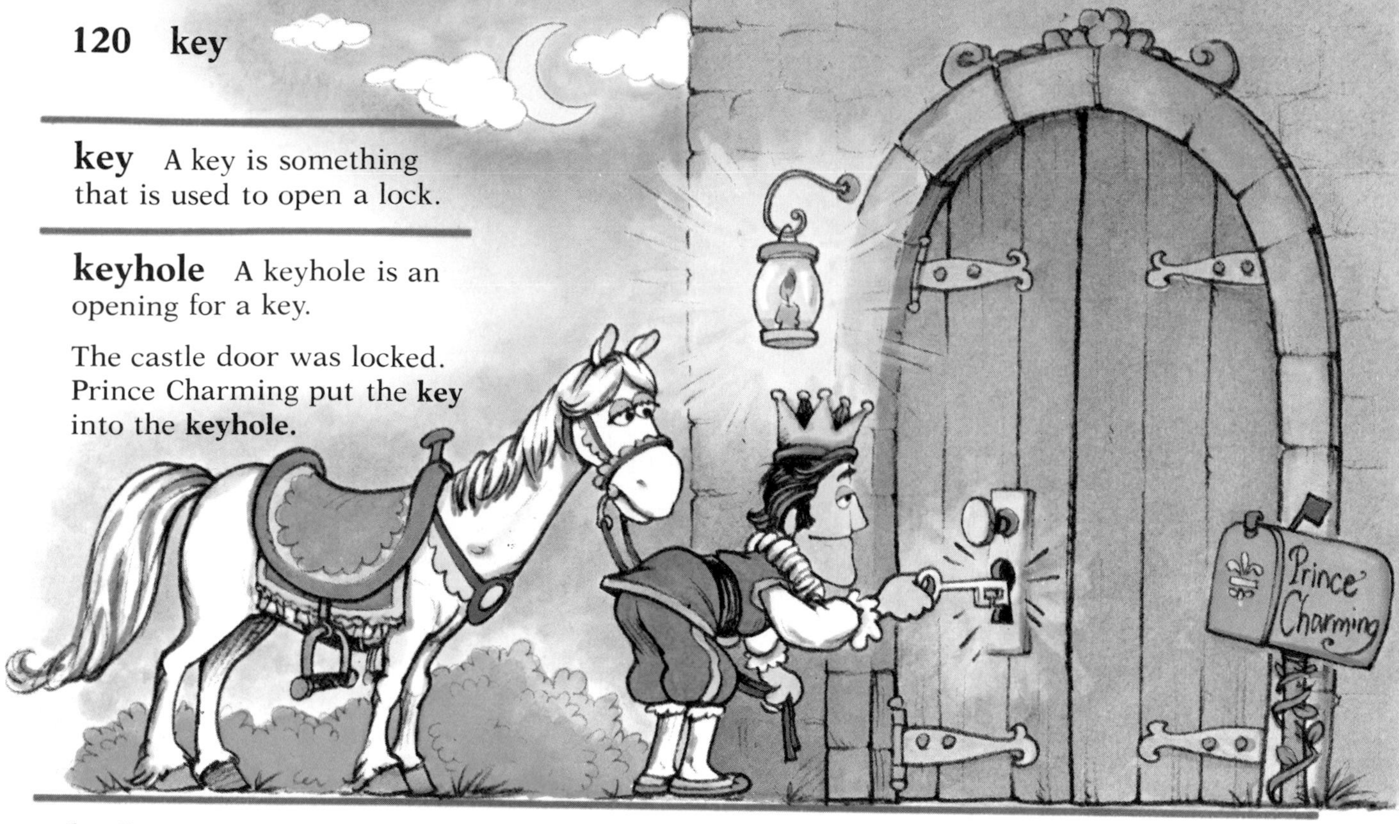

kick When you kick something, you hit it with your foot.

Ernie likes to **kick** his football.

Farmer Grover's cow **kicked** over the milk pail.

kid Kid means young goat. In everyday talk, kid is used to mean child.

Did you know that a **kid** can be a young goat or a child?
You're **kidding**!
Someone who is **kidding** is joking.
KID
KID

kill When you kill something, you make it die.

Wow, I can **kill** seven in one blow!

The little tailor **killed** seven flies with a fly swatter.

kind When you are kind, you are friendly and helpful.

Big Bird dropped his groceries.
Betty Lou helped him pick them up.
That was a **kind** thing to do.

kind Kind also means sort or type.

What **kind** of sandwich would you like, sir?
I'll have a peanut butter and jelly sandwich.
What **kind** of peanut butter — crunchy or plain? What **kind** of jelly — grape or gooseberry? What **kind** of bread ...
This is ridiculous! Just bring me an ordinary peanut butter and jelly sandwich on a plate.
Very well, sir! What **kind** of plate?

kindergarten Kindergarten is the class at school that comes before first grade.

Farley is helping the **kindergarten** teacher. He is passing out the scissors and paste.

king A king is a man who rules a country.

King Cookie is sitting on his throne.

Me proclaim today National Cookie Day!
Cookies

kiss When you kiss, you touch a person with your lips. A kiss shows love or friendship.

Betty Lou is going to **kiss** Grover.

kitchen A kitchen is a room where food is cooked.

Bert is in the **kitchen** cooking oatmeal.

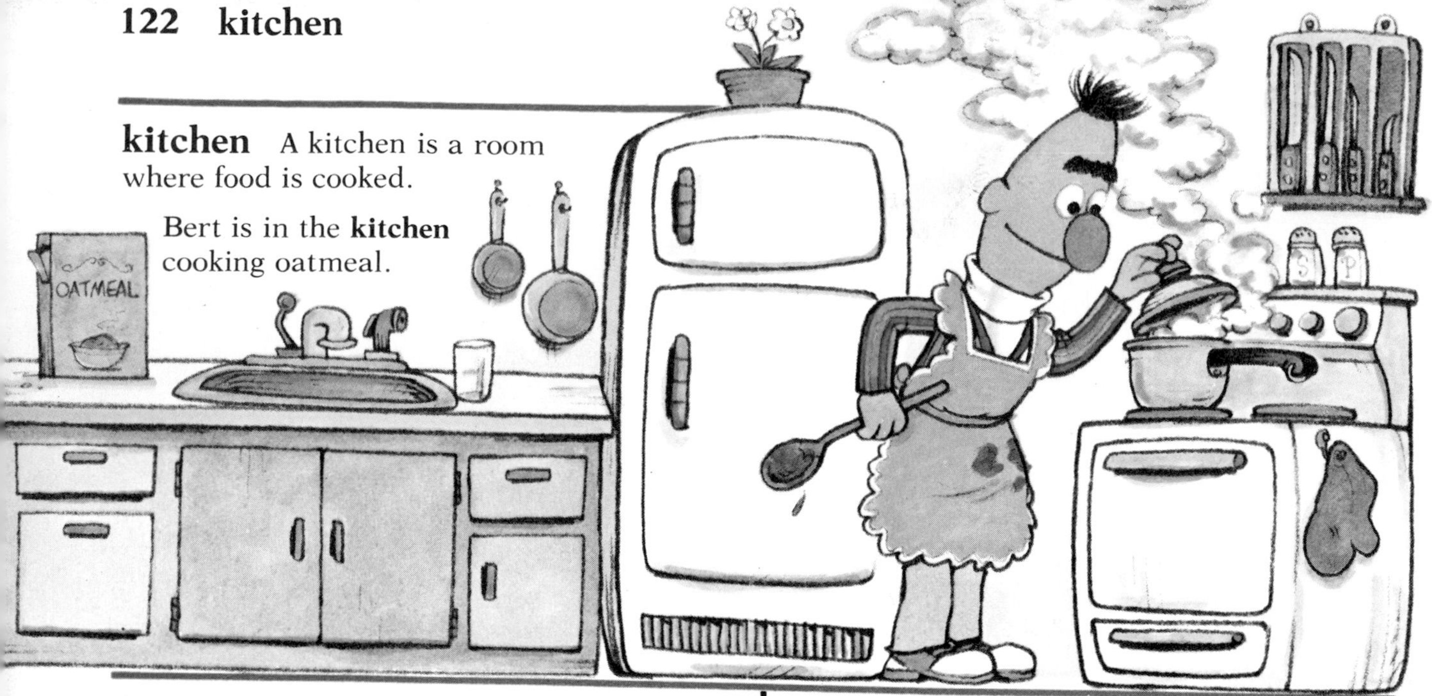

kite A kite is a toy made of paper, plastic, or wood. It flies in the air on the end of a long string.

Big Bird is flying a **kite.**

kitten A kitten is a young cat.

My cat, Fatatatita, has **kittens.** Not only are they adorable, but I can count them. 1, 2, 3, 4, 5, 6... six **kittens**!

knee The knee is the middle part of your leg. Your leg bends at the knee. Look up the word body.

Betty Lou has a bandage on her **knee.**

knife A knife is a tool that is used to cut things. It has a handle and a blade.

Waiter! This **knife** does not cut very well. Please bring me something a little sharper.
Right away, sir!

knock When you knock, you hit your knuckles against something to make a noise.

Herry Monster is going to **knock** on Betty Lou's door.

Next time, Herry, don't **knock.** Use the doorbell.

knot A knot is made by tying together pieces of one or more ropes, ribbons, or strings.

know When you know something, you are sure of it.

Farley **knows** his address.

koala A koala is a small furry animal with big ears and no tail. A koala looks like a little bear, but it is not a bear.

A B C D E F G H I J K L M N O P Q R S T U V W X Y Z

ladder A ladder is something that you can climb to reach high places. A ladder has steps that are called rungs.

Fire fighter Ernie is climbing a **ladder.**

lake A lake is water with land all around it. A lake is larger than a pond.

Prairie Dawn is paddling her canoe on the **lake.**

land Land is the part of the earth that is not water. Another word for land is ground.

I can travel on **land**...
On water...
And in the air.

land When something lands, it comes down to the ground.

Grover's airplane is going to **land.**

language Language is what we use to say things to other people. When two people understand each other's words, they know the same language.

Cookie Monster can say COOKIE in five different **languages.**

Biscotto

large Large means big.

Marshal Grover ordered a small glass of milk for himself and a **large** glass of milk for Fred.

last When something is last, it comes after all the others.

Cookie Monster is the **last** in line. He wishes he were first.

late When you are late, you come after the time that you were supposed to.

You're **late** for our party, Connie!
I'm sorry. I couldn't find my broom.
HAPPY HALLOWEEN

late Late can also mean near the end.

The party ended **late** at night. Everyone had a good time.

later Later means after now.

Hey, Bert! Do you want a banana?

laugh When you laugh, your whole face smiles and you make ha-ha sounds.

laundry Laundry is all the clothes that need to be washed or the clothes that have just been washed.

Ernie and Bert are doing their **laundry.**

lay When you lay something down, you put it down.

Bart **laid** his cards on the table.

lazy Someone who is lazy does not want to work or to play.

The cat and the pig and the mouse are **lazy.**

lead When you lead, you show others the way by going with them or in front of them.

leader A leader is someone who leads.

I, Sherlock Hemlock, will **lead** you out of the woods.
Sherlock Hemlock is our **leader.** Follow him.
TOWN →
← DEEP WOODS

leaf A leaf is a thin, flat green part of a tree or a plant. It grows at the end of a branch or a stem.

A cabbage **leaf** is the **leaf** that I like best. Cabbage **leaves** are delicious.

learn When you learn, you find out something that you did not know before.

I had to **learn** to use a lasso.
I am **learning** how to use a lasso, too.
I have a lot more to **learn.**

leave When you leave, you go away.

When you leave something behind, it does not go with you.

When you leave something alone, you do not touch it or bother it.

Come on, Bert. It's time to **leave** for the show.
Do you think we should **leave** these cookies here?
Leave them alone, Ernie. We don't have time to put them away.

LATER

left When something is left, it is still there after all the others are gone.

Cookie Monster ate almost all of the cookies. There is only one **left.**

left Left is also a direction. It is the **opposite** of right.

Now let me see. Should I turn **left** or right?
If I were Goldilocks, I would turn around and go home.
HOUSE of the THREE BEARS
HOUSE of the BIG BAD WOLF
LEFT
RIGHT

leg Your leg is the part of your body between your hip and your foot. Look up the word body.

Bert's **legs** are longer than Ernie's **legs.**

Ernie, I think you are wearing my pants.

length The length of something is how long it is from one end to the other.

The **length** of this straw is eight inches.

The **length** of a story is its number of pages or how much time is needed to read or tell it.

Look up the word inch.

less Less means not as much.

I have **less** milk than Bart has.
I have the **least** amount of milk.

let When you let something happen, you allow it to happen.

Let the balloon fly away!
Okay. I **let** it go.

letter A letter is a mark that stands for a sound. There are twenty-six letters in the alphabet. You can put letters together to make words. Look up the word alphabet.

letter A letter is also a message that you write on paper and give or mail to someone.

I, the Amazing Mumford, will now pull from this perfectly empty hat two different things that have the same name.
A LA PEANUT BUTTER SANDWICHES!
L

librarian A librarian is someone who works in a library.

library A library is a room or building where books are kept. You can borrow books from a library.

Farley went to the **library.** The **librarian** helped him find a book about dragons.

lick When you lick something, you touch it or taste it with your tongue.

Lasso Louise likes to **lick** luscious lollipops.

Say that ten times, fast.

lid A lid is a cover.

The **lid** to Oscar's garbage can is on his head.

lie When you lie, you rest on your stomach or back or side.

Barkley likes to **lie** near Big Bird's nest.

lie A lie is something that is not true.

Hey, Bert, there's a big ugly monster with two heads and four arms and eight legs, and he's standing right behind you.
You can't scare me, Ernie. I know that's a big **lie.**

Gee, Bert, how did you know I wasn't telling the truth?
Because the monster is standing behind *you,* not me!

lift When you lift something, you pick it up.

Herry Monster can **lift** a crane.

A crane can **lift** Herry Monster.

light When there is light, it is not dark and you can see. Something that gives light is sometimes called a light.

In the daytime, the sun gives us **light.**
At night, when it is dark, we can turn on electric **lights.**

light When you light something, you set it on fire.

Mommy, after you **light** the candles on my birthday cake, I will blow them out.
Make a wish first, dear.

light When something is light, it is not heavy.

A feather is **light.** It is easy to carry.
A big rock is heavy. It is not easy to carry.

lightning Lightning is a flash of light you see in the sky.

Sometimes there is **lightning** during a rainstorm.

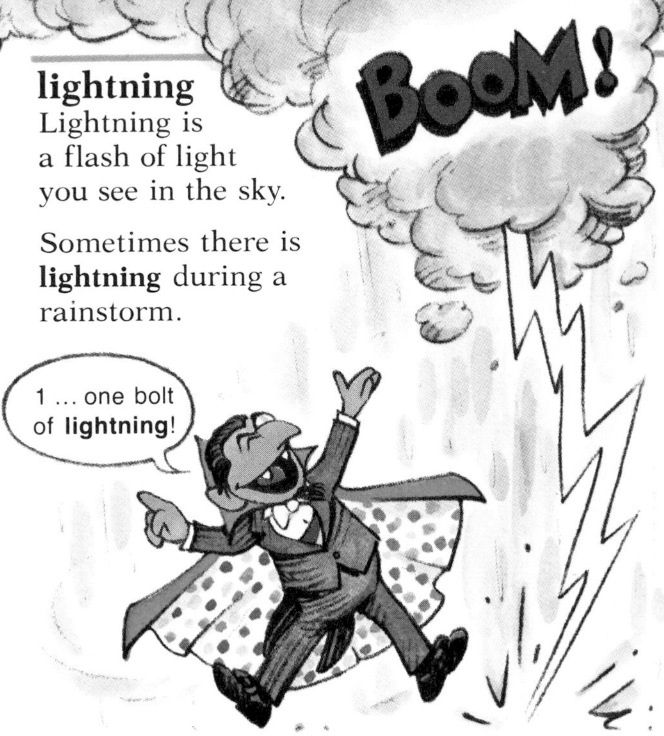
BOOM!
1 ... one bolt of **lightning**!

like When you like someone or something, that person or thing makes you feel good.

I really **like** Rubber Duckie.

like When one thing is like another thing, they are the same in some way.

What is **like** a big red furry monster with horns?
Another big red furry monster with horns!

line A line is a long, thin mark.

Lines can be straight or curved or wiggly or crooked.

line When people or things are in a line, they are behind or next to each other. They are in a row.

There is a **line** of people waiting to see the new movie.

TICKETS

lion A lion is a big, wild cat that roars.

I am a baby **lion.** I am a cub.
I am the cub's mother. I am a **lion**ess.
I am the cub's father. I am a **lion.**

A group of **lions** is called a pride. Grown-up male **lions** have manes. **Lion**esses do not.

liquid A liquid is something that is wet and can be poured.

Three of these things belong together.
One of these things is not the same.

Orange juice, milk, and water are all kinds of **liquids.** A loaf of bread is not wet and cannot be poured.
The loaf of bread does not belong.

listen When you listen, you pay attention to the sounds you hear.

Hey, everyone! **Listen** to Little Jerry and the Monotones.

little Something that is little needs less room than something that is big. It is small, not large.

How do you become a big hairy monster?
You start out as a **little** hairy monster—and then you grow!

live To live somewhere means to have your home in that place.

CTW
SESAME STREET
SLIMEY
I **live** in a garbage can. Slimey **lives** in a box. We both **live** on Sesame Street.

lock A lock is something that keeps something else from being opened. You usually need a key to open a lock.

lock When you lock something, you fasten it with a lock.

Sherlock Hemlock always **locks** his trunk with a big **lock.**

lonely When you feel lonely, you wish you had someone to be with.

It's **lonely** at the top.

long When something is long, the beginning is far from the end.

When something takes a long time, there is a lot of time between the beginning and the end.

It took me a **long** time to learn to use my lasso.
L

Lasso Louise has a **long** lasso.

look When you look, you pay attention to the things you see.

A detective has to **look** for clues.

loose When something is loose, it is not tight.

Farley put on his father's shoes. They are **loose.**

lose When you lose something, you cannot find it.

Did you **lose** something, Big Bird?
Yes, I **lost** the key to this lock.

I, Sherlock Hemlock, the world's greatest detective, will find the key with my trusty magnifying glass.
But first I must find my trusty magnifying glass. Where did I put that thing?
Did you **lose** it?

lost When something is lost, you cannot find it.

LOST AND FOUND DEPT.
LOST:
one key to Big Bird's lock
and
one trusty magnifying glass

loud When something is loud, it makes a lot of sound.

That's too **loud,** Oscar!
What?
BANG!
BANG!
I said, THAT'S TOO **LOUD,** OSCAR!
If you'd stop yelling, Betty Lou, we could have some peace and quiet around here.

love When you love someone, you care about that person very much.

I **love** you, Mommy.
I **love** you, too, Grover, dear.
Sometimes when you like something very much, you say you **love** it.
I just **love** carrots.

low Something that is low is close to the ground.

lunch Lunch is the meal that you eat in the middle of the day.

Biff and Sully are going to eat **lunch.** Biff's **lunch**box is empty.

Mm

A B C D E F G H I J K L **M** N O P Q R S T U V W X Y Z

machine Machines are built by people to do special kinds of work.

This machine makes mud.
DIRT 100% PURE
I'm mad. I'm really mad.

mad When you are mad, you do not like what has happened. You are angry.

magic Magic is a way of doing something that seems to be impossible. Magicians, witches, and fairies use magic to make amazing things happen.

I, the Amazing Mumford, will make this monster disappear.
A LA PEANUT BUTTER SANDWICHES!
That is magic!

Amazing Mumford the **magician** does **magic** tricks.

mail Mail is the letters and packages that are sent from one place to another.

Big Bird is dropping his **mail** into the **mail**box.

The **mail** carrier is putting the **mail** into his **mail**bag.

The **mail** carrier is delivering the **mail** to Granny Bird.

make Make means to put together or cause something to happen.

Cookie Monster loves to **make** cookies. Today he **made** twelve cookies and one mess.

make-believe When something is make-believe, it is imaginary. It is not real.

We are not real bears. We are only **make-believe.**

man A man is a grown-up boy.

There is one **man** in the elevator.

many Many means a lot of people, things, or animals.

There are **many** monsters in the elevator.

map A map is a special kind of picture that shows where places are.

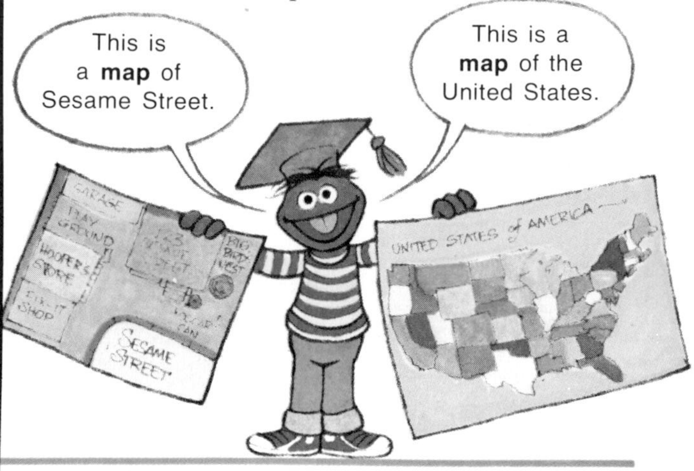

This is a **map** of the United States.

march When you march, you walk with rhythm in steps of the same size.

I want to see the Monster **Marching** Band **march** down Sesame Street.

mark A mark is a line, spot, dent, or sign on something. A mark can be made by accident or on purpose.

I made a **mark** on the map to show where we live.
Ernie, who made this crayon **mark** on our new table?

marry When two people marry, they become husband and wife.

The monsters are getting **married.**

Will you **marry** me?
Why not?
I now pronounce you husband and wife.
I just love weddings!

mask A mask is something you wear over your face.

Farley and Betty Lou are wearing **masks.**

Trick or treat!

match A match is a thin stick with a special end that is used to make a flame.

I never play with **matches. Matches** can be dangerous.

match When two things match, they are the same in a certain way.

THE MATCHING GAME!
And now folks, it's time for— THE **MATCHING** GAME! Each one of our contestants is holding a shape. All you have to do is find the shapes that **match.**

may May means allowed to.

Cookie Monster, you **may** have one cookie.
COOKIES

maybe Maybe means possibly.

Maybe Grover is in the yellow box or **maybe** Grover is in the red box.
FIND THE BOX THAT GROVER IS IN.

me Me is a word you use when you are talking or thinking about yourself.

Surprise! Here I am. You did not find **me**!
FIND THE BOX

meal A meal is all the food that is served when it is time to eat. You usually eat three meals a day—breakfast, lunch, and dinner.

My favorite **meal** is meat loaf and mashed potatoes and carrot salad.
My favorite **meal** is moldy bread and rotten eggs and stinkweed salad.
AAGGGHH! Some **mean** person put carrots in my salad. Where is my stinkweed?

mean When someone is mean, that person does or says things that are not kind or friendly.

mean What you mean is what you want to show by your words or your actions.

Grrmmphh!
What do you **mean,** Oscar? I don't understand.
That's grouch talk. I **mean** go away and leave me alone.

measure When you measure something, you find out how long or how heavy or how much it is.

I can **measure** my height.
I can **measure** my weight.
I can **measure** a cup of flour for baking cookies.
FLOUR

mechanic A mechanic is someone who uses tools to make or repair machines. Look up the word tool.

The Count's car is broken. The **mechanic** is trying to fix it.

meet When you meet someone, you get together with that person.

I'm happy to **meet** you.

melt When something melts, it turns to liquid.

It is a warm day. The snow monster is starting to **melt.**

medicine When you are sick, you sometimes use medicine to make you well.

Take your **medicine,** dear, like a good monster!

mess When things are dirty or out of place, we say they are a mess. When something is a mess, it is not neat.

I don't know anyone who can make a bigger **mess** than you, Oscar.
Gee thanks, Betty Lou. That's the nicest thing you've ever said to me.

metal Metal is the hard stuff that some things are made of. Iron, gold, silver, and tin are kinds of metal.

Keys are made of **metal.**

Coins are made of **metal.**

Cans are made of **metal.**

middle The middle is the place between the beginning and the end. The middle is also the place that is the same distance from all the sides. It is the center.

Three people are standing at the milk bar. Marshal Grover is in the **middle.**

Big Bird drew a circle with chalk. Little Bird is standing in the **middle.**

midnight Midnight is twelve o'clock at night.

Dum de dum de dum. Time for my **midnight** snack!

milk Milk is a liquid food that comes from cows and other animals. Milk is good to drink.

Farmer Grover's pail is full of **milk.** He has just **milked** his cow.

mind Your mind thinks and knows and remembers and feels.

Everyone at the bus stop is thinking of something different. Three different **minds** are thinking three different thoughts.

BUS STOP

To **mind** means to care.
Do you **mind** if I borrow your dictionary?

mine Mine means belonging to me.

This towel is yours. The other towel is **mine.**

minute A minute is a small amount of time. There are sixty seconds in a minute. There are sixty minutes in an hour.

Waiter, you have exactly one **minute** to bring my milk.
Whoa, Bossie!

minus Minus means take away or subtract.

3-1=2
Three **minus** one is two.

mirror A mirror is a glass in which you can see yourself.

Egad! A suspicious-looking person! I wonder who he is.
Sherlock, that is *you* in the **mirror.**

miss When you miss something, you do not hit it or find it or meet it or see it or hear it.

Keep your eye on the ball, Ernie, or you'll **miss** it.

Hurry, Sherlock, or you will **miss** the train.
I can't leave now. I'm looking for my **missing** ticket.

miss When you miss someone, you feel sorry that person is not with you.

What's the matter, Big Bird?
I **miss** Mr. Snuffle-upagus.

mistake When you make a mistake, you do something wrong.

I think we made a **mistake,** Sully.

mitten A mitten is a cover for your hand to keep it warm. A mitten has a place for your thumb and a place for your other fingers.

Farley is wearing red **mittens.**

mix When you mix things, you put them together.

You **mix** the potion while I read the recipe. Let's see... two toadstools, three bat wings...

money Money is what we use to buy things.

Hey, kid. Would you like to buy an M? It costs only nine cents.
I don't have enough **money.** I have only six cents.

You're in luck. That's exactly what this wonderful W costs.
?

monkey A monkey is a hairy animal with two arms and two legs. Most monkeys have long tails.

Do you know what is more fun than a barrel of **monkeys**?
Counting the **monkeys** in a barrel!

monster A monster is a large or strange living thing.

The **monsters** on Sesame Street are furry and friendly.

month A month is an amount of time that lasts about thirty days. There are twelve months in a year. Each month has a special name.

Thirty days hath September,
April, June, and November.
All the rest have thirty-one,
Excepting February alone,
And that has twenty-eight days clear,
And twenty-nine in each leap year.
ALMANAC

moon The moon is the earth's closest neighbor in space. You can sometimes see it in the sky.

Isn't the **moon** beautiful?

Grover the astronaut is on the **moon.**

Isn't the earth beautiful?

mop A mop is made of yarn or sponge that is fastened to a long stick. A mop is used for cleaning floors.

Bert is using a **mop** to **mop** the floor.

more More means a larger amount.

You have **more** cookies than I do, Ernie.
That's true, Bert. But Cookie Monster has **more** cookies than *I* do. He has the **most.**

morning The morning is the first part of the day.

RING!
Oh! Time for my **morning** snack.

mother A mother is a woman who has a child.

Grover's **mother** is reading a bedtime story to Grover.

Once upon a time...

motor A motor is an engine.

Grover Knover's **motor**cycle has a **motor.**

mountain A mountain is a part of the earth that is higher than the land around it.

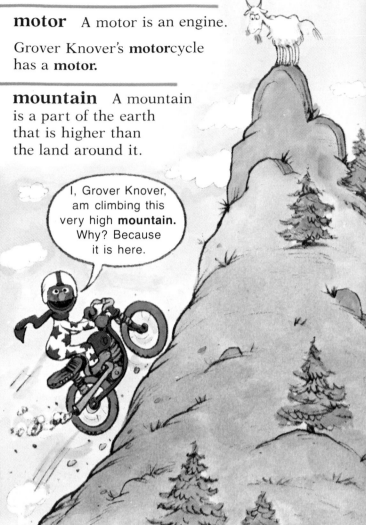

I, Grover Knover, am climbing this very high **mountain.** Why? Because it is here.

mouse A mouse is a small, furry animal with a long tail.

If you have one **mouse**...
And someone gives you another **mouse**...
You have two **mice.**

mouth Your mouth is a part of your face. You eat, drink, and speak through your mouth. Look up the word face.

Hello, everybod-ee! I am here to tell you about the **mouth.** I am using my **mouth** to talk.

move When you move, you go from one place to another place.

When you move something, you take it from one place to another place.

Sometimes the word move is used to mean changing the place where you live.

The **movers** are **moving** the country mouse to the city.
I think I'd like to **move** to the city.
CHEEZY MOVERS INC.
Ernie, let's **move** to another seat. I can't see the movie.
Prairie, please **move** your coat so I can sit in that seat.
That's not my coat. It's Cookie Monster sleeping.
ZZZ

movie A movie is moving pictures that you watch on a screen. A movie usually tells a story.

Bert and Ernie are watching a **movie.**

much Much means a great amount.

THE SESAME STREET THEATER
NOW PLAYING
THE COUNTRY MOUSE MOVES TO THE CITY
Did you like the **movie,** Bert?
I liked it very **much.**
EXIT

mud Mud is soft, wet dirt.

Who stepped in my box of **mud**?
Don't worry, Oscar. I will solve the mystery. I will look for someone with **muddy** shoes.
FRESH MUD

muscle A muscle is a part of your body that can stretch and pull tight to make your body move. You have many muscles inside your body.

Herry Monster uses his **muscles** to lift the barbell.

music Music is pleasing sound that is played or sung by people. Different people like different kinds of music.

Everyone at the party is listening to the **music.**

Stop making that terrible noise!
Terrible noise? This is **music** to my ears.

must Must means have to.

I **must** find the person who is wearing muddy shoes. Then I will know who stepped in Oscar's mud box.

my My is another way of saying belonging to me.

Egad! **My** shoes are covered with mud. *I* am the person who is wearing muddy shoes.

I'll just sit down here and clean them off.
FRESH MUD

myself Myself is a word that is sometimes used instead of me or I.

mystery A mystery is something that you do not understand and try to figure out.

I found the mud on my shoes. I, **myself,** am the one who stepped in your mud box, Oscar. The **mystery** is solved.
Good, because I have another **mystery** for you to solve. Someone *sat* in my mud box.
FRESH MUD

Some of my favorite M words are missing from this dictionary— messy, moldy, and mushy. Do you know what I wish? I wish *I* were missing from this dictionary.

nail A nail is a long, thin piece of metal that can be hammered into wood.

Prairie Dawn is making a wagon.

This **nail** will hold two pieces of my wagon together.

nail Your nails are the hard coverings that grow on the ends of your fingers and toes.

Biff is cutting his **nails.**

name A name is the word you use for a person, place, or thing.

Hi! My **name** is Miss Muffet. This is my pet spider. His **name** is Stanley.

nap When you take a nap, you sleep for a small amount of time.

Snuffle-upagus is taking a **nap.**

narrow Narrow means not wide.

Sully, that board is too **narrow.** Find one that's wider.

near Near means close to.

Marshal Grover is **near** the cactus. Fred is far away.

neat Neat means not messy.

Ernie's closet is messy.

Bert's closet is **neat.**

ERNIE'S CLOSET
BERT'S CLOSET
Ernie, I think you have my scarf around your **neck.**

neck Your neck is the part of your body between your head and your shoulders. Look up the word body.

need When you need something, you cannot do without it.

needle A needle is a long, thin tool used for sewing. A needle has a small hole at one end and a sharp point at the other.

Super Grover **needs** a **needle** and thread to sew up a hole in his cape.

neighbor A neighbor is someone who lives near you.

neighborhood Your neighborhood is the place where you and your neighbors live.

We are all **neighbors.** We all live in the same **neighborhood.**
HOOPER'S STORE
1 2 3

nephew If you are a boy, you are your aunt and uncle's nephew.

She is my aunt. He is my uncle.
He is our **nephew.**

nest A nest is a thing made by birds or other animals to hold their babies.

A baby bird must learn to fly before it leaves its **nest.**

never Never means not at any time.

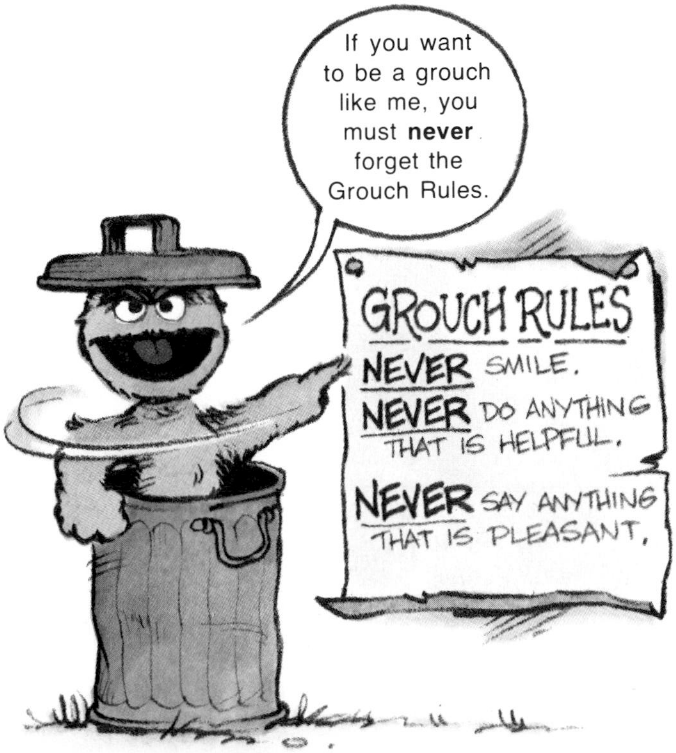
If you want to be a grouch like me, you must **never** forget the Grouch Rules.
GROUCH RULES
NEVER SMILE.
NEVER DO ANYTHING THAT IS HELPFUL.
NEVER SAY ANYTHING THAT IS PLEASANT.

new When something is new, it has just been made or has never been used.

Goldilocks broke Baby Bear's chair.

CRUNCH!

Papa Bear made Baby Bear a **new** chair.

newspaper A newspaper is one or more sheets of paper printed to tell about the new things that have happened.

Did you hear the **news**? Sherlock Hemlock found a needle in a haystack.
Yes, I read about it in the **newspaper.**
NEWS
SHERLOCK HEMLOCK FINDS PROVERBIAL NEEDLE IN HAYSTACK!

next Next means nearest to or beside.

next Next also means the following one.

Betty Lou is standing **next** to Farley.
We missed the bus. We'll have to take the **next** one.
BUS STOP

nice Something that is nice is pleasing.

Everyone likes Barkley because he is a **nice** dog.

nickel A nickel is a coin. A nickel is worth five cents. Look up the word coin.

Each of the Busby twins has five cents.

I have a **nickel.**
I have five pennies.

nickname A nickname is a special name that you use in place of a real name.

His real name is the Amazing Mumford, but I call him Mumphie.
Mumphie is my **nickname.**

niece If you are a girl, you are your aunt and uncle's niece.

She is my aunt. He is my uncle.
She is our **niece.**

night Night is the time of day when it is dark. Night starts when the sun sets and ends when it rises.

Grover sleeps with his teddy bear every **night.**

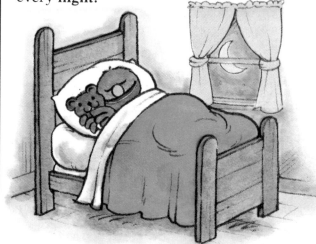

nine Nine is a number. Nine is one more than eight.

The Count has **nine** candles on his piano.

nineteen Nineteen is a number. Nineteen is ten plus nine more.

Bert has ten Figgy Fizz bottle caps and nine Prune Crush bottle caps in his collection. He has **nineteen** bottle caps all together.

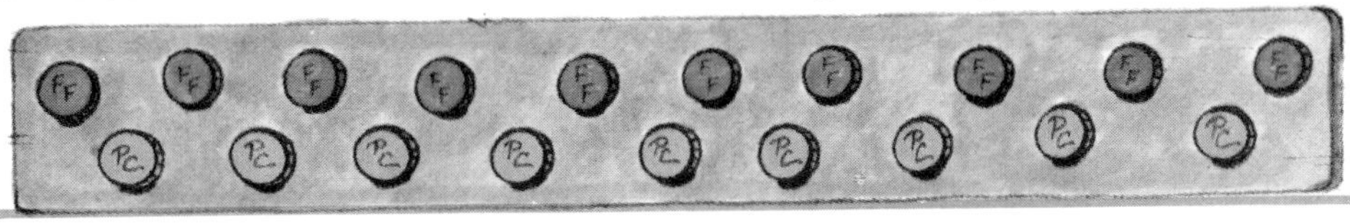

no No means not true or wrong. No also means you will not or cannot do something. No can also mean not any.

Is your name Goldilocks?
No!
Hey, Bert, do you want to play football?
No!
Do you have any bananas?
No. I have no bananas today.
APPLES

noise Noise is sound that is not pleasing to hear.

He is making a loud noise!

none None means not any.

There were three bats in my belfry. They all flew away. Now there are none.

noon Noon is the middle of the day. At noon it is twelve o'clock.

SESAME GULCH DEPOT
It is **noon.** The twelve o'clock train is on time.

nose Your nose is a part of your face. You use your nose to breathe and smell. Look up the word face.

Grover is smelling a flower with his **nose.**

I love flowers. They smell so nice.

nothing Nothing means not anything.

As you can see, there is **nothing** in my hat.

not Not means in no way.

I love stinkweed. Stinkweed does **not** smell nice. It smells terrible. That is why I love it.

now Now means at this time.

Do you want to go out to play, Bert?
Not **now,** Ernie. I'll play later.

number A number tells how many.

I have two plates.
I have two carrots.
I have two kittens.

Each monster has the same **number** of things.

nurse A nurse is someone who takes care of people when they are sick.

Farley went to the school **nurse.** He took Farley's temperature.

nut A nut is a dry fruit or seed that is covered by a hard shell.

Walnut
Pecan
Almond
Cashew
Chestnut
Pistachio
Coconut
Oscar, here is my favorite kind of food that begins with the letter N—**nuts**!
And here is my favorite kind of garbage that begins with the letter N—**nut**shells.

A B C D E F G H I J K L M N **O** P Q R S T U V W X Y Z

oatmeal Oatmeal is a cereal made from oats.

Bert likes **oatmeal.**

ocean An ocean is a very large body of salt water.

Prairie Dawn is sailing her boat on the **ocean.**

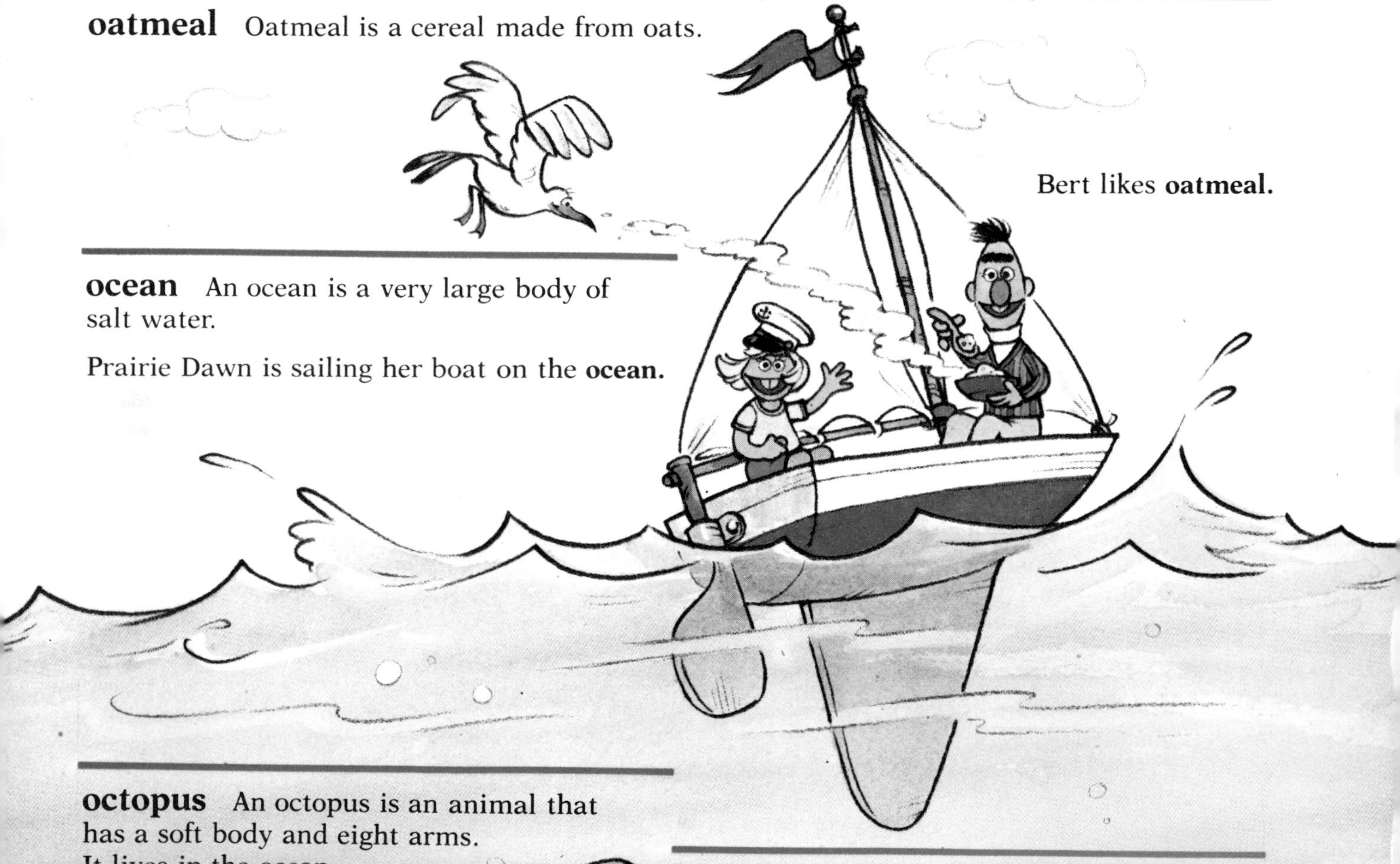

octopus An octopus is an animal that has a soft body and eight arms. It lives in the ocean.

odd Odd is a word that means different or strange.

This **odd** fish is looking at the **octopus.**

of Of means coming from or belonging to.

Half **of** the pie is missing.

of Of also means containing or made from.

I have a loaf of bread, a jar of peanut butter, and a bottle of milk for our picnic. What do you have, Ernie?
I have this sign, Bert.
KEEP OFF THE GRASS
PEANUT BUTTER
MILK

off Off means not on.

off Off also means not in use.

Ernie, you can turn off the radio. The Pigeon News is over.
THE DAILY BORE
Z Z Z z z

office An office is a place where people work.

Farley's mother is president of the Tick Tock Clock Company. She is working in her **office.**

Mommy, do you know what time it is?
PRESIDENT

often Often means again and again.

Herry Monster **often** breaks things.

I can't help it.

old When something is old, it is not new.

How do you like these **old** rags?
Old also means how long someone has lived. I am five years **old.**

on On means touching or covering.

Marshal Grover is **on** his horse, Fred.

on On also means not turned off.

Shhh, Ernie. I'm listening to the radio. The Pigeon News is **on.**
ZZZZ

once Once means one time.

How many times did Barkley bark?
He barked **once.**

one One is a number. When you count, you begin with the number one.

only Only means by itself or no more than.

There is **only** one Cookie Monster.
Thank goodness! This is my **only** cookie.

open Open means not closed.

The door is **open.**

open When you open something, you uncover, unfold, unlock, or remove a part of it.

Ernie had to **open** his door... so he could **open** his mailbox... so he could **open** his letter.

opposite Two things that are opposite are as different from each other as they can be.

Big is the **opposite** of little.

Little is the **opposite** of big.

We are sitting **opposite** each other.
Opposite also means on the other side of.

or Or means one but not the other.

orange An orange is a round fruit that grows on an orange tree.

Farley, do you want a grapefruit or an **orange**?
I want an **orange.**

Orange is also the name of a color.
Look up the word color.

orchestra An orchestra is a large group of musicians playing different kinds of musical instruments together.

The Amazing Mumford is leading the **orchestra.**

ostrich The ostrich is the largest bird in the world. It cannot fly but can run very fast.

Hey, Big Bird, the dictionary says that the **ostrich** is the largest bird in the world.
Oh, yeah?

other Other means not the same as the one being talked about.

There is only one meatball on this plate. I ordered two meatballs. Where is my **other** meatball?
Here is your **other** meatball, sir.

our Our means belonging to us.

This is **our** bicycle. The bicycle is **ours.**

out When something is out, it is not in.

Betty Lou is in the cannon!

Betty Lou is **out** of the cannon!

outdoors When you are outdoors, you are not in a building.

Bert is indoors.

Ernie is **outdoors.**

outside Outside means not inside.

What are you doing **outside** your nest?
I'm painting the **outside** of my nest today.

oven An oven is a closed space where things can be baked. An oven can be part of a stove.

Cookie the baker bakes bread in an **oven.**

over Over means above.

The Amazing Mumford waves his magic wand **over** his hat.

over Over also means again.

The trick didn't work, Mumphie. Do it **over.**
?

over Over also means the other side up.

If you don't turn your hat **over**, Mumphie, nothing can come out.
!

over Over also means finished.

The Amazing Mumford's magic show is **over.**

own When you own something, or something is your own, it belongs to you.

I **own** two broken umbrellas. Aren't they wonderful?

There is only one great O word. Can you guess what it is?
OSCAR

A B C D E F G H I J K L M N O **P** Q R S T U V W X Y Z

package A package is a bundle or a box with something inside. Sometimes a package is wrapped in paper and taped or tied with string.

Hey, Bert, here's a **package** for you!
Nifty, Ernie! My pigeon T-shirt finally came.

page A page is a piece of paper in a book, a magazine, or a newspaper.

Everything I've ever wanted to know about pigeons is in this book, Bert.
But, Ernie—the **pages** in that book have nothing on them.
That's right, Bert. That's all I want to know about pigeons—nothing! Hee hee hee.

paint Paint is used to color or protect things. Paint is wet when you put it on something, and then it dries.

Biff and Sully are using green **paint** on the wall.

pair A pair is two things that go together.

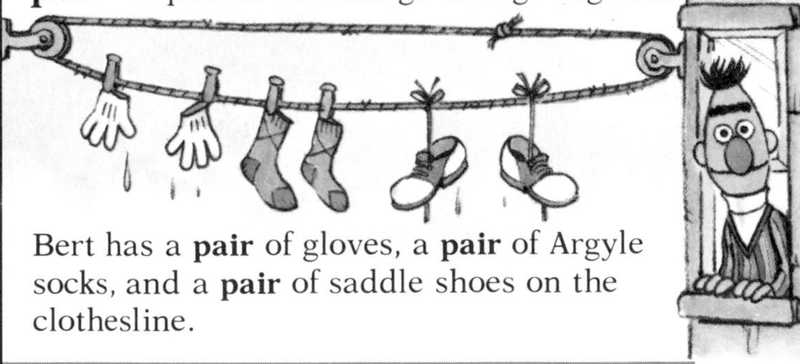

Bert has a **pair** of gloves, a **pair** of Argyle socks, and a **pair** of saddle shoes on the clothesline.

pajamas Pajamas are clothes to sleep in.

Prairie Dawn is ready for bed. She is wearing her **pajamas.**

YAWN!

pal A pal is a good friend.

palace A palace is a very large and fancy house.

Prince Charming lives in a **palace.**

pan A pan is a metal or glass dish that is used for cooking.

Cookie Monster is frying an egg in a **pan.**

pants A pair of pants is clothing you wear over your hips and legs.

Bert cannot decide which pair of **pants** to wear.

paper Paper is flat and thin and is used to write and paint on. Paper is also used for wrapping packages and covering walls.

Three of these things belong together.
One of these things is not the same.

The **paper** airplane, the news**paper,** and the magazine are made out of **paper.** The frying pan is made out of metal. The frying pan does not belong.

parade A parade is a group of people who are marching together—usually to music.

What is blue and red and purple and green and comes down the street making a lot of noise?
The Monster Day **parade**!

parent A parent is a mother or a father.

I'm her mother.
I'm her father.
They are my **parents.**

park A park is a place outdoors where people can have fun. Sometimes a park has a playground in it.

Bert likes to feed the pigeons in the **park.**

part When you have a part of something, you have some but not all.

I have a whole apple.
Now I have **part** of an apple.
YUM!

party A party is a group of people having fun together.

pass When you pass something, you go by it.

HOOPER'S STORE
We **pass** Mr. Hooper's store on our way to school.

paste Paste is something you use to make things stick together.

I am using **paste** to **paste** these pictures into my scrapbook.
PASTE

pat When you pat something, you touch it gently.

PAT THE DOG PLEASE!

patch A patch is a piece of cloth or other material that is used to cover a tear or a hole.

There is a **patch** on Super Grover's cape.

path A path is a narrow trail that people or animals walk on.

Little Red Riding Hood is walking on the **path** to grandmother's house.

GRANNY'S

pay When you pay for something, you give money for it.

I will **pay** you fifty pennies for sweeping the floor.
Then I will **pay** you fifty pennies for a new bag of marbles.
MARBLES
MARBLES
MARBLES 50¢
MARBLES

pea A pea is a little, round green vegetable. Peas grow in pods on vines.

peach A peach is a round fruit with fuzzy skin and a pit in the middle. Peaches grow on peach trees.

peanut A peanut is a vegetable that grows under the ground. The seed inside the shell is good to eat.

pear A pear is a fruit with smooth skin. Pears grow on pear trees.

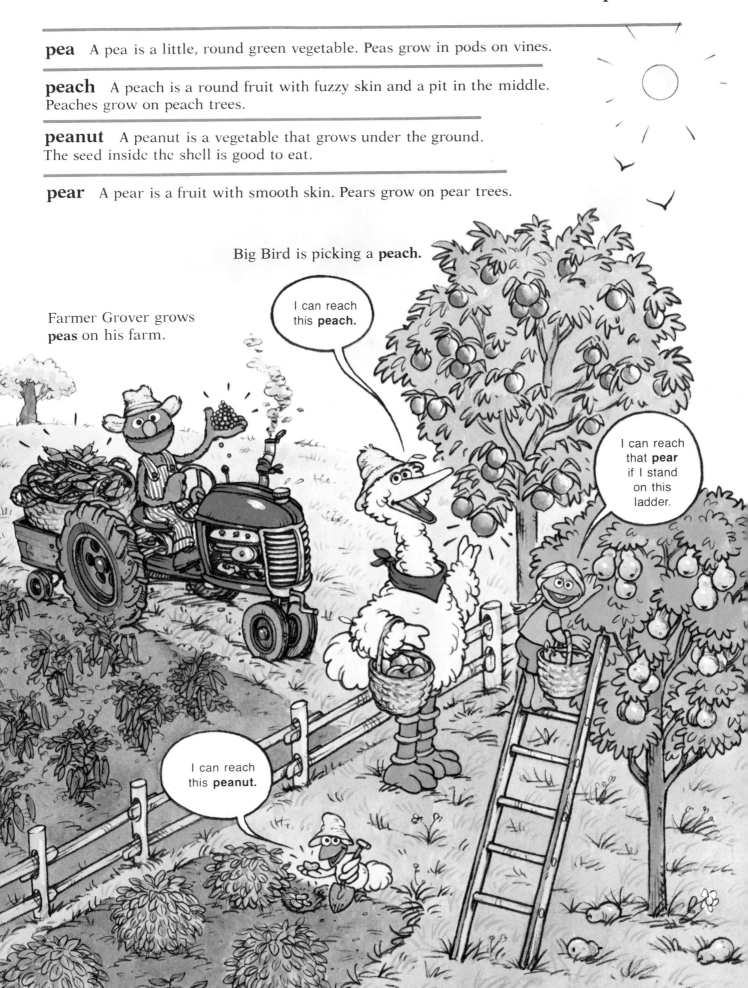

Big Bird is picking a **peach.**

Farmer Grover grows **peas** on his farm.

I can reach this **peach.**
I can reach that **pear** if I stand on this ladder.
I can reach this **peanut.**

pebble A pebble is a small stone. A pebble is usually smooth and round.

This **pebble** will be great for my **pebble** collection.

peek When you peek at something, you look quickly.

Get ready! I am going to let you **peek** at Slimey.

pen A pen is a tool used for writing or drawing with ink.

I can write my name with a **pen.**

pencil A pencil is a tool used for writing or drawing. A pencil mark can be erased.

I can write my name with a **pencil.**

penny A penny is a coin. A penny is worth one cent. Look up the word coin.

I have six **pennies.**
I have one nickel and one **penny.**

Each of the Busby twins has six cents.

people Children, women, and men are people.
These are some of the **people** in Big Bird's neighborhood.

perfect When something is perfect, it cannot be better.

Sam the robot makes mistakes. Sam is not **perfect.**

person A person is a child, a woman, or a man.

pet A pet is an animal that is loved by the person who takes care of it.

photograph A photograph is a picture taken with a camera. The person who takes the picture is called a photographer.

The **photographer** is taking a **photograph** of Bert and his **pet,** Bernice.

piano A piano is a musical instrument with white and black keys that you press with your fingers.

Don Music is playing the **piano.**

pick When you pick something, you pull it away with your fingers.

Betty Lou likes to **pick** flowers.

pick Pick also means choose.

picnic A picnic is a meal that is eaten outdoors.

I brought my favorite food to the Grouch Day **picnic**— sardines with chocolate sauce.
GROUCH DAY PICNIC

picture A picture shows how something looks. A picture can be a photograph, a painting, or a drawing.

This is a **picture** of me when I was a baby.

pie A pie is something to eat. Most pies are round and have a crust on the outside and a filling on the inside.

What does Frazzle Monster like to put in his **pies**?
His teeth!
GRUNT! GRUNT!
SLURP!

piece A piece is one part of something.

I want a **piece** of pie.

pig A pig is an animal with four legs, a short nose called a snout, and a curly tail.

Farmer Grover is feeding his **pigs.**

I am a baby **pig.** I am called a **pig**let.
I am the **pig**let's mother. I am a sow.
I am the **pig**let's father. I am a boar.

pigeon A pigeon is a bird with a small head, a chubby body, and short legs.

Bert loves his **pigeon,** Bernice. Bernice loves Bert.

pile A pile is a group of things lying on top of each other.

Here is a **pile** of dirty laundry. I will wash it.
Here is a **pile** of clean laundry. I will fold it.

pillow A pillow is a bag filled with something soft. You can rest your head on a pillow.

Cookie Monster, do you know what a **pillow** is for?
Sure, Betty Lou. You sleep on a **pillow.**
I thought you were going to say you eat it, Cookie Monster.
!
That good idea! Mmmm ... Delicious!

pilot A pilot is someone who flies an airplane. A pilot is also someone who steers a ship.

I'm an airplane **pilot.**
I'm a **pilot** on a ship.
S.S. SESAME

place When you know where, you know the place.

My favorite **place** is a pond—with ducks and frogs and lily pads.

My favorite **place** is the dump.

pin A pin is a short, thin piece of metal used to fasten things together.

This is a straight **pin.**
This is a safety **pin.**

plain Something that is plain is not fancy or decorated.

Sometimes I like to wear a **plain** hat.
Sometimes I like to wear a fancy hat.

plan When you plan, you decide what you are going to do before you do it.

plant A plant is any living thing that is not an animal. Trees, flowers, and grass are kinds of plants.

plant When you plant a seed, you put it in dirt.

Sam the robot is watering the **plants.**

plate A plate is a flat dish.

Monster dinners are really great! We eat the food—and then the **plate**!

play When you play, you do something that is fun.

Big Bird likes to **play** hide-and-seek with Snuffle-upagus.

play When you play a musical instrument, you make music.

Bert likes to **play** his accordion.

play A play is a story that is acted on the stage.

The Sesame Street **Players** are performing a **play.**

please Please is a friendly word to use when you ask someone to do something for you.

plenty When you have all that you need, you have plenty.

plum A plum is a small, round fruit with smooth skin and a pit in the middle. Plums grow on plum trees.

These **plums** are ripe. They look yummy.

plumber A plumber is someone who knows how to fix the water and gas pipes in a building.

The **plumber** came to Farley's house to fix the kitchen sink.

plus Plus means added to.

Two **plus** one is three.
2
+1
3

pocket A pocket is a place in your clothes where you can put things.

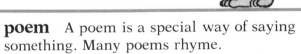

Prairie Dawn likes to keep her pet lizard in her **pocket.**

poem A poem is a special way of saying something. Many poems rhyme.

Mary had a little lamb. Its fleece was white as snow. And everywhere that Mary went, the lamb was sure to go.
Poems
YA!

point A point is the sharp end of something.

The witch's hat has a **point.**

point When something points, it shows the way.

poison Poison is something you should not eat or drink because it can make you sick or can kill you.

When I see one of these pictures on something, I know it means poison, and I should stay away.

pole A pole is a long, narrow piece of wood or metal.

Grover is painting the flag**pole.**

police officer A police officer is a person whose job is to make sure people obey laws.

Mr. Police Officer, can you tell me how to get to Sesame Street?
Sure. Right after I give you a ticket for not stopping at that red light.

pond A pond is a small body of water. A pond is bigger than a puddle and smaller than a lake.

Farmer Grover likes to swim in the **pond** with his ducks.

pony A pony is a small horse.

Prairie Dawn likes to ride her **pony.**

pool A pool is a pond or a special place made for people to swim in.

Betty Lou likes to dive into the swimming **pool.**

poor Poor means not having enough money to buy the things you need.

I always send birdseed to my cousin Bartholomew because he is too **poor** to buy it for himself.
BIRD-SEED

poor Poor also means unlucky or unhappy.

Poor Bert. He is all out of oatmeal.
OAT-MEAL

popcorn Popcorn is a special kind of corn that pops when it is heated.

The Count is popping **popcorn.**

... four hundred and ninety-three ... four hundred and ninety-four ... Oh, I love to count the pops!

porcupine A porcupine is a small animal covered with stiff, sharp hairs called quills.

I wonder why some people say that a **porcupine** is like a big pin cushion.
PRESS
Oh!

possible When something is possible, it can be done.

Is it **possible** that someone brave and smart and strong will hear us calling for help and come to our rescue?
It is **possible.** I can help them.

post office A post office is a place where people can buy stamps, mail letters and packages, and pick up their mail.

Marshal Grover went into the **post office** to mail a letter to his mother.

pot A pot is a deep, round container. Some pots are for cooking and some are for planting flowers in.

Oscar is growing stinkweed in a flower**pot.**

potato A potato is a vegetable that grows in the ground.

Farmer Grover is digging up a **potato** for his dinner.

Farmer Grover is baking the **potato** in the oven.

pour When you pour something, it flows from a container.

power Power is energy or strength to do something.

practice When you practice, you do something over and over until you can do it better.

Big Bird is learning to use a lasso. He needs to **practice** more.

present A present is something nice you give to someone for a special reason.

Granny Grouch sent me a **present** for my birthday. I hate **presents.**
Hey, great! It's just what I wanted. A banana peel! Granny Grouch always picks the right color, too. Heh, heh.

pretend When you pretend, you make believe or imagine.

Bert, you **pretend** to be Little Bo Peep and I'll be your sheep.
You look silly in that sheep costume, Ernie.

pretty When something is pretty, it is pleasing to look at.

price The price of something is how much it costs.

Pamela Monster is trying on a **pretty** hat.

What is the **price** of this hat?

prince A prince is the son of a king and a queen.

princess A princess is the daughter of a king and a queen.

I am the king.
I am the queen.
I am the **princess.**
I am the **prince.**

prize A prize is a reward for winning or doing something.

Cookie the baker won a **prize** for the best cookie.

Your cookie is delicious!
Your **prize** is delicious!

problem A problem is something that is difficult to do or a question that is hard to answer.

How will I get out of here?

Biff has a **problem.**

promise When you promise to do something, you agree to do it.

I **promise** to take good care of your plants while you are away.

protect When you protect someone, you keep danger away.

Don't worry! I will **protect** you.

proud When you feel proud, you feel good about yourself.

When I help people, I feel **proud.**

pudding Pudding is a soft cooked food. It is usually sweet and is eaten as a dessert.

Mr. Smith wants **pudding** for dessert.

I'll have rice **pudding** ...
No, I'll have bread **pudding** ...
No, I'll have chocolate **pudding** ...
No, I'll have tapioca **pudding** ...

puddle A puddle is a small pool of water on the ground.

Big Bird likes to step in **puddles** when he is wearing his boots.

pull When you pull something, you take hold of it and move it toward you.

Farmer Grover is trying to **pull** his mule into the barn.

push When you push something, you make it move away from you.

Betty Lou is trying to **push** Farmer Grover's mule into the barn.

puppet A puppet is a doll that moves when you pull its strings or put it on your hand.

I want you to meet my **puppets,** Crummy and Yucchy.

put When you put a thing somewhere, you place it there.

Mr. Chatterly is going to **put** his chair next to the fireplace.

puzzle A puzzle is a toy with pieces that fit together.

This is my favorite **puzzle.**

puppy A puppy is a young dog.

The **puppy** is following its mother.

It's no picnic being in this dictionary! I have to put up with all those dumb words like party, play, please, present, and pretty. I can't stand it!

Q q

A B C D E F G H I J K L M N O P **Q** R S T U V W X Y Z

quarter A quarter is a coin. A quarter is worth twenty-five cents. Look up the word coin.

Each of the Busby twins has twenty-five cents.

I have a **quarter.**

I have twenty-five pennies.

quarter A quarter is one of four equal parts of something.

Zounds! A **quarter** of the pie is missing!

queen A queen is a woman who rules a country. A queen can also be the wife of a king.

The **queen** is sitting on her throne.

I proclaim today National Be Kind to Grouches Day!

Aaggh!

question A question is what you ask when you want to know something.

Do you have any sardine ice cream with pickles?

The answer to that **question** is no.

quick Quick means fast.

That brown fox is **quick.**

quiet It is quiet when there is no noise.

At last it is **quiet** and I can get some sleep.

The Q section went quickly— but not quickly enough. I have just one question.

When are you going to turn the page so I can quit looking at you?

Rr

A B C D E F G H I J K L M N O P Q **R** S T U V W X Y Z

rabbit A rabbit is a furry animal with long ears.

race A race is a contest to see who is the fastest.

The **rabbits** are about to have a **race.**

BIG RACE TODAY!
RABBITS ONLY!
TORTOISES UNWELCOME!
FINISH
On your mark ... Get set ...
1ST PRIZE

radio A radio is a machine. When you turn on a radio, you can hear music or voices.

Bert is listening to the Pigeon News on the **radio.**

Today, Peter Pigeon was seen eating birdseed on the corner of Main Street and Third Avenue.

railroad A railroad is a track for trains. A track is made with long metal strips called rails.

Look up the word train.

The **railroad** workers are working on the **railroad.**

rain Rain is water that falls in drops from clouds.

rainbow A rainbow is a strip of colors that you sometimes see in the sky when it rains.

raincoat A raincoat is a coat that keeps you from getting wet when it rains.

rake A rake is a tool used to make the ground smooth or clear.

Big Bird is using a **rake** to **rake** away the leaves.

ranch A ranch is a place for raising animals.

Rodeo Rosie lives on a **ranch.**

raw Food that is raw is not cooked.

Rodeo Rosie gives her horse **raw** carrots to eat.

reach When you reach, you stretch out a part of your body to take or touch something.

Cookie Monster can **reach** the cookie jar on the top shelf.

When are we going to **reach** the next restaurant?
Reach also means to arrive at a place.
FOOD FUEL 5 MI.

read When you read, you understand the words you see.

I
can
read
I ... can ... **read.**

I
can
read
I can **read**!

ready If you are ready to do something, you have everything you need to do it.

Hey, Bert! Are you **ready** to go to the costume party?
I'm **ready.**

Bert is not a **real** pigeon.
Bernice is a **real** pigeon.

real Real means true. A real thing is not make-believe.

really Really means truly.

That's a **really** scary monster costume you are wearing.
This is not a costume. I **really** am a monster.

reason When you know why something happens, you know the reason.

Give me a **reason** why I should believe you are a real witch.
Oh!

recipe A recipe tells you how to make something to eat.

record A record is a round, flat piece of plastic that can be played on a record player to make music.

rectangle A rectangle is a shape with four sides and four square corners.

Three of these shapes are **rectangles.**
A circle is not a **rectangle.**
The circle does not belong.

refrigerator A refrigerator is a machine that keeps food cold.

relative Your relatives are the people in your family.

remember When you remember, you think of something that happened in the past.

rent When you rent something, you pay to use it. You do not own it.

repair Repair means fix.

Prairie Dawn can **repair** a broken chair.

rest When you rest, you nap or stay quiet for a while.

Big Bird needs to **rest** every afternoon.

rest The rest of something is everything that is left.

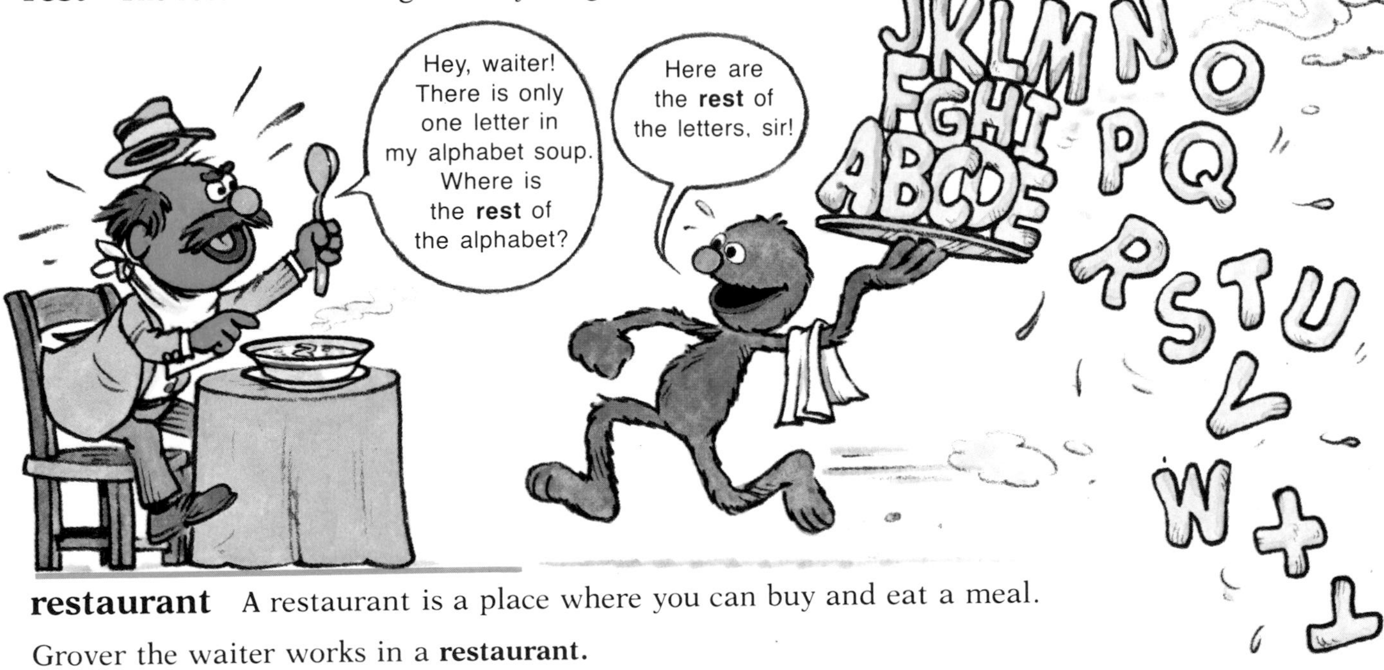
Hey, waiter! There is only one letter in my alphabet soup. Where is the **rest** of the alphabet?
Here are the **rest** of the letters, sir!
JKLMN O FGHI PQ ABCDE RSTU V W X Y

restaurant A restaurant is a place where you can buy and eat a meal.

Grover the waiter works in a **restaurant.**

return When you return, you come back after being away. When you return something, you give it back.

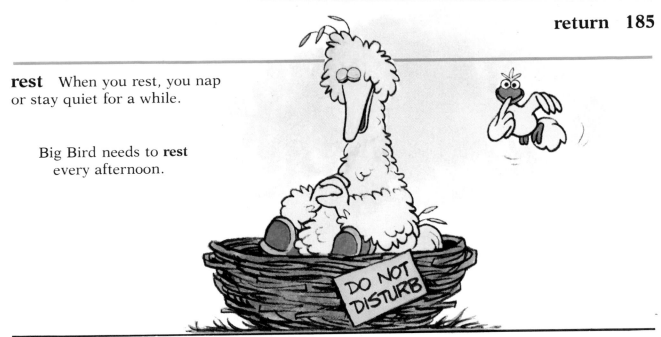

I wonder when Ernie will **return.**
Sorry I'm late, Bert. I had to **return** the hammer I borrowed from Biff.

rhinoceros A rhinoceros is a big animal with thick skin and one or two horns on the top of its nose.

rhyme Words that rhyme sound alike at the end.

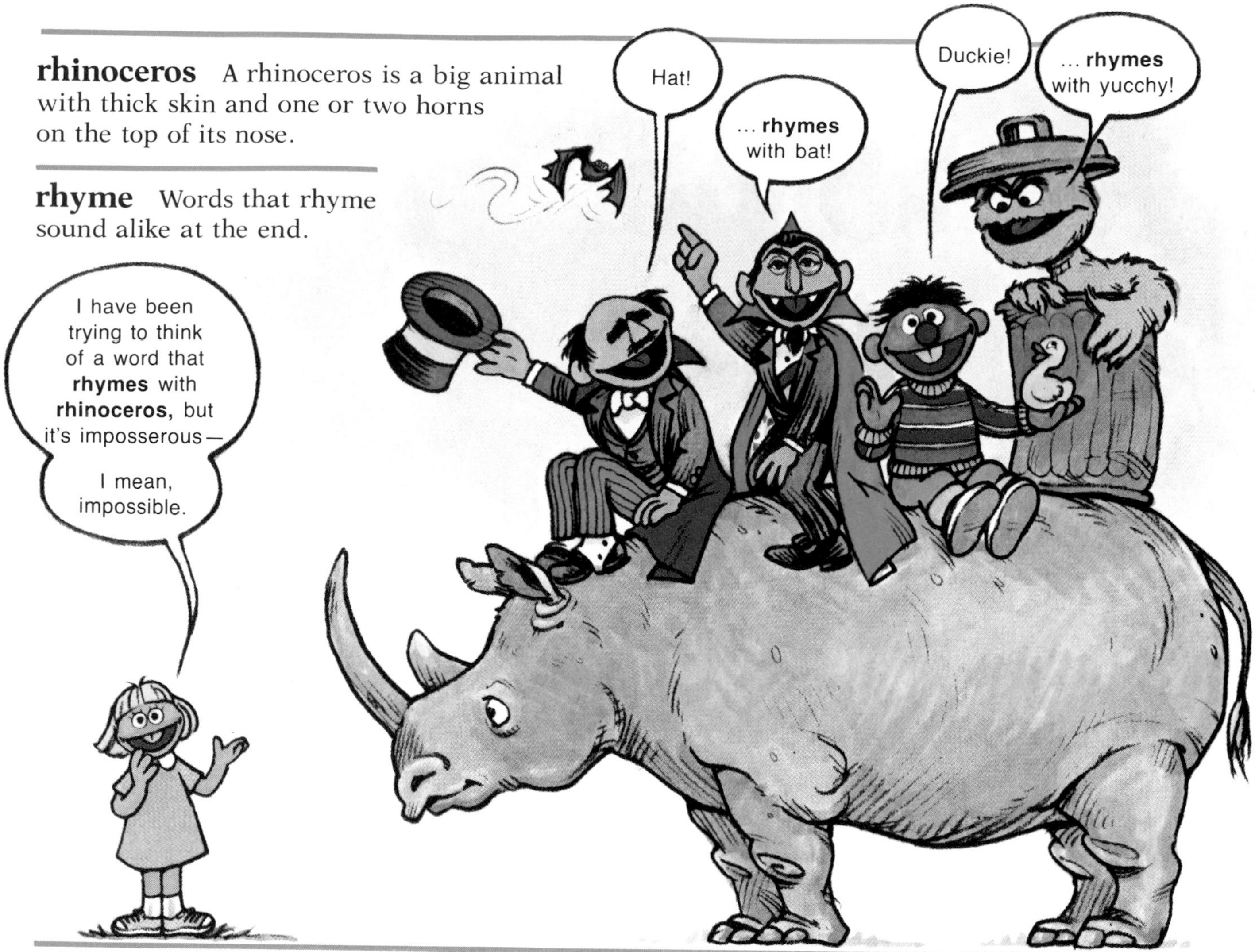
I have been trying to think of a word that **rhymes** with **rhinoceros,** but it's imposserous—
I mean, impossible.
Hat!
... **rhymes** with bat!
Duckie!
... **rhymes** with yucchy!

ribbon A ribbon is a narrow piece of cloth or paper.

Bert tied a **ribbon** around his present for Ernie.

rice Rice is a kind of grain. Rice grows above the ground in shallow water. Some cereals are made from rice.

Betty Lou is picking **rice.**

rich When you are rich, you have lots of money.

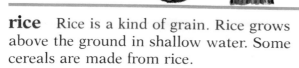

Gourmet
OATMEAL
IMPORTED
"FOR THE DISCRIMINATING PALATE"
JUMBO SIZE!
If I were **rich,** I would buy the biggest box of oatmeal in the whole world.

riddle A riddle is a question that is also a puzzle.

ride When you ride, you sit or stand while something carries you along.

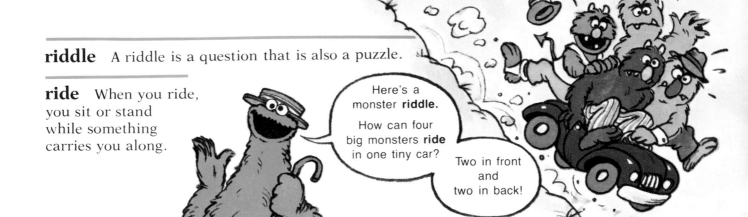

Here's a monster **riddle.**
How can four big monsters **ride** in one tiny car?

Two in front and two in back!

right When something is right, it is correct. It is not wrong.

Grover, you had two big boxes, and I gave you two more. Now you have four big boxes. **Right?**
That's **right**!

ring A ring is a circle.

Rodeo Rosie is in the center of the **ring.**

Ring around a Rosie ...
A **ring** that you wear is a circle that fits around your finger.

right Right is also a direction. It is the opposite of left.

This is my **right** hand.
This is my **right** foot.
Right away means at once or immediately.

ring When something rings, it makes the sound of a bell.

Three of these things belong together.
One of these things is not the same.

A telephone, a cowbell, and a bicycle bell are things that **ring.** A banana does not **ring.** The banana does not belong.

river A river is a large stream of water that flows into another river, a lake, or an ocean.

Prairie Dawn is paddling her canoe up the **river.**

Down by the **river**side ...

road A road is a man-made path between two places. It is wide enough for automobiles and trucks to ride on.

The Count is driving his bat car along the **road.**

robot A robot is a machine that can follow orders to do certain kinds of work.

Sam the **robot** can do many things that people can do.

rock A rock is a piece of stone. A rock is hard and comes out of the ground.

I found a nice **rock** for your collection, Bert.

rock When you rock, you move back and forth or from side to side.

Farley likes to **rock** in a **rocking** chair.

rocket A rocket is a machine that moves through the air or up into space. Sometimes rockets go to the moon or other planets.

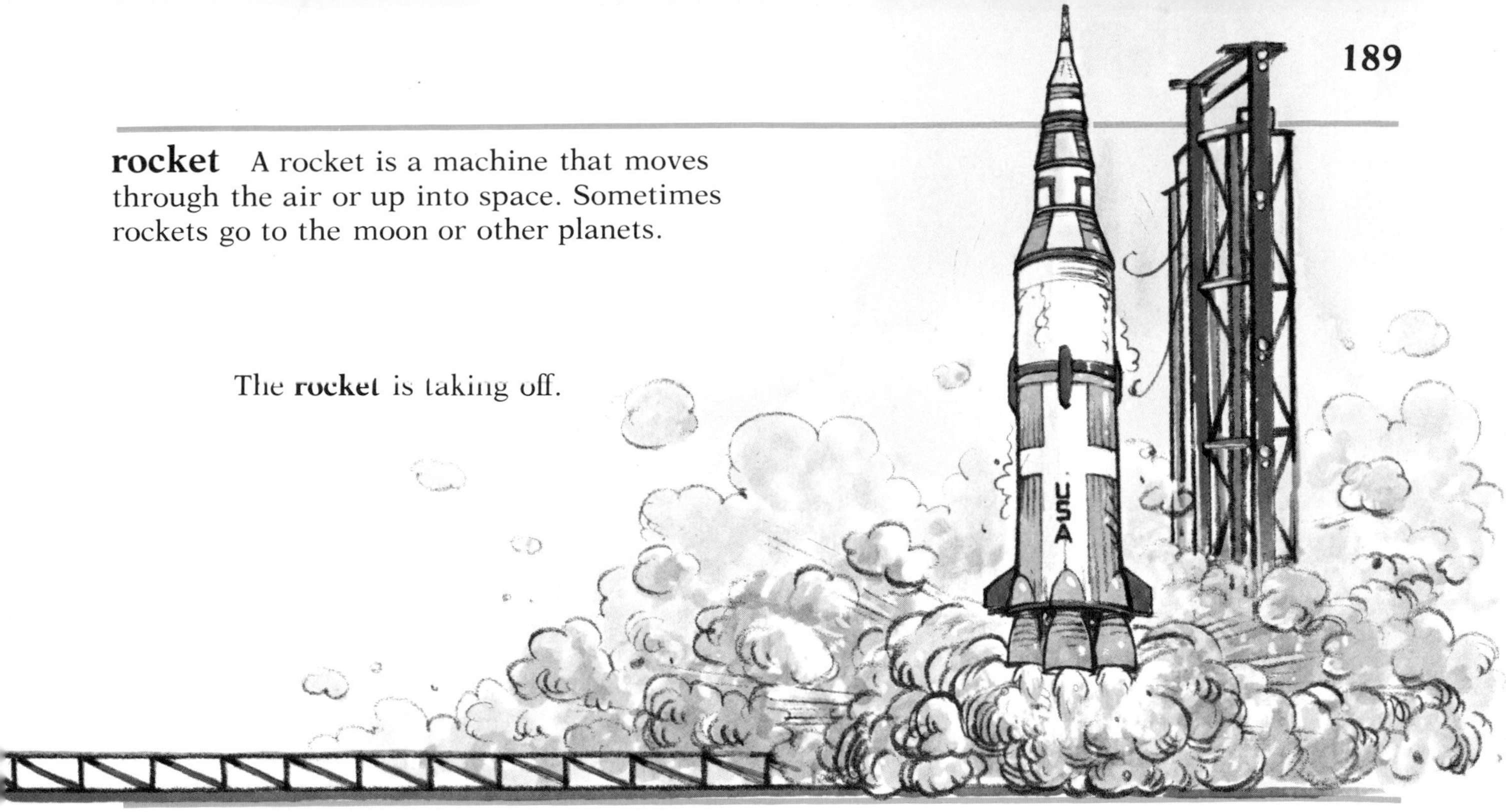
USA

The **rocket** is taking off.

rodeo A rodeo is a show in which cowgirls and cowboys ride horses and rope steers.

Come and see the **rodeo**!

roll When something rolls, it turns over and over as it moves along.

Betty Lou's ball started to **roll** down the hill, and Barkley chased it.

roof A roof is the top covering for a building.

Biff is fixing the **roof.**

NAILS

room A room is space inside a building. A room is surrounded by walls.

This **room** belongs to my cat, Fatatatita.
FATATATITA

root A root is the part of a plant that is under the ground. Plants take in food through their roots. Some roots can be eaten.

rope A rope is a strong, thick cord that can be used to tie things together.

Herry Monster forgot to untie the **rope.**

rough Rough means not smooth.

This ground is very **rough** and bumpy.

round Something round is shaped like a ball or a circle.

Three of these things belong together.
One of these things is not the same.

An orange, a ring, and a wheel are **round.**
A book is not **round.**
The book does not belong.

row A row is a line of people or things.

There is a **row** of birds on Bert's clothesline.

row When you row, you move a boat by pulling oars through the water.

Herry likes to **row** his **row**boat.

rubber Rubber is something that stretches and is waterproof. Many things are made out of rubber.

Rubber boots.
Rubber ball.
Rubber band.
Rubber Duckie.

rug A rug is a cover for the floor. A rug can cover the whole floor or a part of it.

Bert likes to vacuum the **rug.**

ruler A ruler is a tool with straight edges. It is used for measuring length. Look up the word length.

This board is two feet long.

The carpenter is using a **ruler.**
She is measuring the length of a board.

run When you run, you move very quickly on your feet.

Marshal Grover can **run** fast.
Fred can **run** faster.

Whoa, Fred! Wait for me!

This is ridiculous! How can you have a dictionary without words like rude and rubbish and rotten? I am going to read something *really* interesting.
THE ROTTEN EGG AND I

sad When you are sad, you feel unhappy.

Big Bird is **sad.**
He did not
get a letter from
Snuffle-upagus.

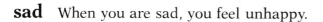

safe Safe means not in danger.

The little pig is **safe.**
The big bad wolf cannot
blow his house down.

sail A sail is a piece of cloth that catches the wind.

sailboat A sailboat is a boat with one or more sails.

Prairie Dawn's
sailboat has
one **sail.**

salt Salt is tiny white grains that come from the ground or from sea water. Some people put salt on food because they like the way it tastes.

Sully is shaking **salt**
on his hard-boiled egg.

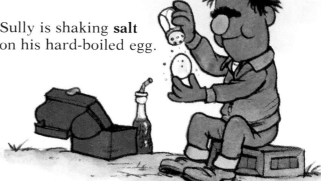

same When things are the same, they are like each other.

Cookie and Grover are wearing the **same** tie.

sand Sand is made of tiny grains of rock. You can find sand in the desert or at the beach.

Betty Lou likes to play in the **sand** at the beach.

sandwich A sandwich is two pieces of bread with some other food in between.

Here is my favorite **sandwich**—sardines and sour pickles on stinkweed bread!

save When you save something, you keep it in a safe place.

Bert **saves** bricks.

save Save also means to rescue someone or something from danger.

Uh-oh! There is someone who needs my help. I will **save** her.

HELP! HELP! Somebody **save** me from this furry blue monster!

saw A saw is a tool. It is made of metal and has teeth for cutting.

Prairie Dawn is cutting a board with a **saw**.

say Say means speak.

Ernie, why are you wearing earmuffs in the house?
What did you **say,** Bert? I can't hear you because I'm wearing earmuffs.

scale A scale is a machine that is used to weigh people or things.

Snuffle-upagus is standing on a **scale.** How much does he weigh?

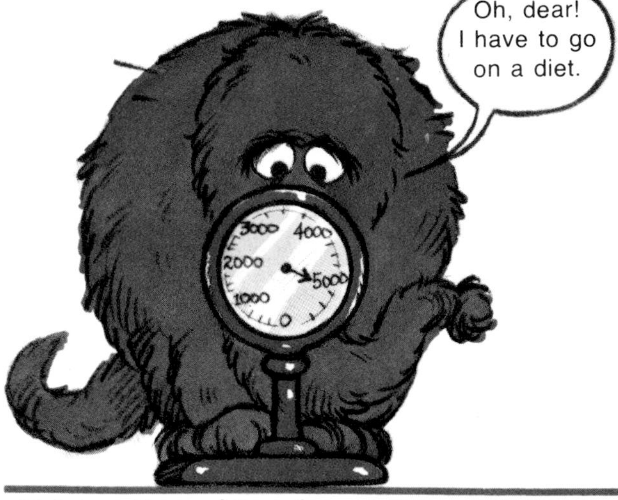

Oh, dear! I have to go on a diet.

scare Something that scares you is something that makes you afraid.

BOO!
Did I **scare** you? Heh, heh, heh.

school A school is a place where you go to learn things from teachers.

When I was a little count, I went to **school** to learn to count.
1 ... one wonderful **school**!
C

scissors Scissors are a tool used for cutting. Scissors have two handles and two blades.

I am cutting out paper birdies with my **scissors.**
Snip
Snip
Snip

scream When you scream, you make a loud noise with your voice.

EEEEEE!
Don't **scream,** Betty Lou. There is nothing to be afraid of. It's only me, Herry.
I'm not afraid. I'm **screaming** because you are standing on my foot.

sea A sea is a very large body of salt water.

I like to swim in the **sea.**
Sea and ocean are two names for the same thing.

season A season is a time of the year.
There are four seasons: winter, spring, summer, and fall.

Farmer Grover works hard every **season.**

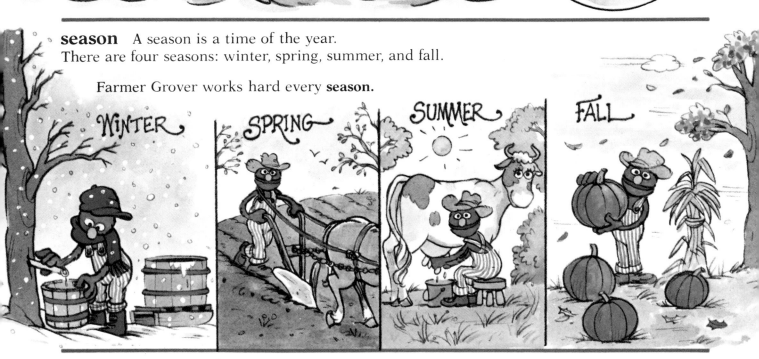

WINTER
SPRING
SUMMER
FALL

seat A seat is something to sit on.

Three of these things belong together. One of these things is not the same.

The stool, the chair, and the bench are all kinds of **seats.** A cactus is not a good thing to sit on. The cactus does not belong.

second A second is a very small amount of time. There are sixty seconds in a minute.

The Count is counting the **seconds** on his bat clock.

second Second also means the one that comes right after the first.

Betty Lou is first in line. Barkley is **second.**

secret A secret is a special thing you know but do not tell.

I have a special hiding place, but you do not know where it is. It is my **secret.**

see When you look at something, you see it.

seed A seed is the special part of a plant that can grow into a new plant.

Farmer Grover plants **seeds** in the spring.

selfish If you are selfish, you care about yourself and not about other people.

Cookie Monster! Don't be **selfish**! The cookies are for everyone.
COOKIES

sell When you sell something, you give it to someone and that person gives you money for it. After you sell something, it does not belong to you anymore.

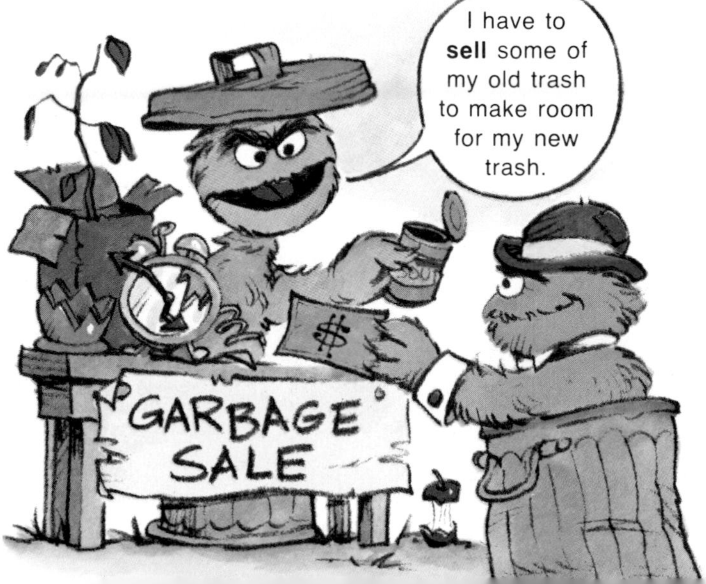

I have to **sell** some of my old trash to make room for my new trash.
GARBAGE SALE

send When you send something, you start it on its way.

I will send a thank-you note to Granny Bird because she sent me some birdseed cookies.

set A set is a group of things that are alike in some way.

I have a set of blue dishes.
I have a set of yellow dishes.

seven Seven is a number. Seven is one more than six.

seventeen Seventeen is a number. Seventeen is ten plus seven more.

Bert has ten red bricks and **seven** gray bricks. He has **seventeen** bricks all together.

sew When you sew, you use a needle to pull thread through cloth or other material. You can sew by hand or by machine.

The Amazing Mumford has to **sew** a new button on his cape.

shadow A shadow is a dark shape. When a light shines on something, it makes a shadow on the other side.

Egad! Look at that shadow on the wall. I think someone is following me.

shake When you shake something, you move it quickly back and forth or up and down.

Ernie has to **shake** the dust out of the mop.

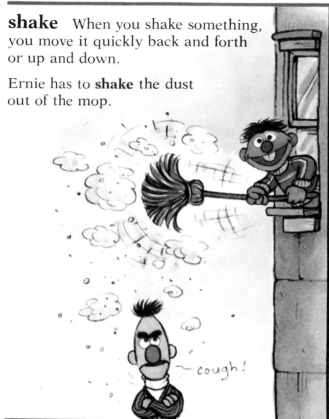

cough!

shape The form of something is its shape.

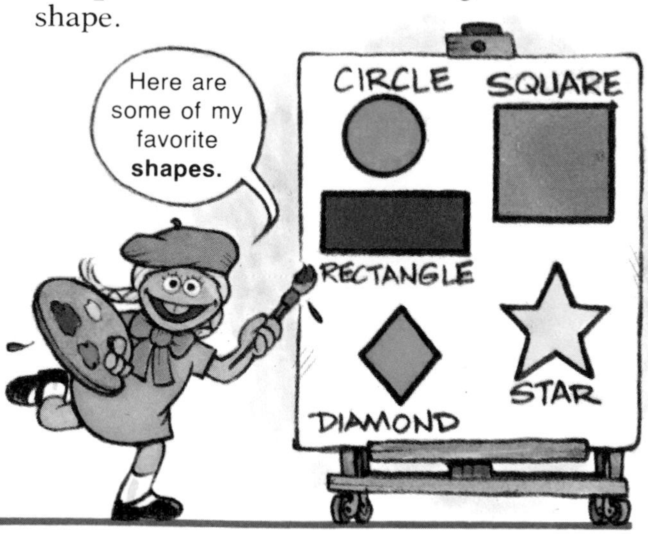
Here are some of my favorite **shapes.**
CIRCLE
SQUARE
RECTANGLE
DIAMOND
STAR

share When you share something, you let others use it or have part of it.

Here, Sully. I will **share** my sandwich with you if you will **share** that apple with me.

shallow Something that is shallow is not deep.

The water in this wading pool is too **shallow** for swimming.
Not if you are a little bird.

sharp Something that is sharp has a thin cutting edge or a point on the end.

Hey, you! Wanna buy this knife? It's so **sharp,** it will cut, peel, slice, chop, saw....
I don't want to buy a knife. But how much is all that wonderful garbage??

she She is another way to say woman or girl or female animal.

Prairie Dawn is busy. **She** is making a home for her pet spider.

sheep A sheep is an animal that has four legs and is covered with wool.

I am a baby **sheep.** I am a lamb.
I am the lamb's mother. I am a ewe.
I am the lamb's father. I am a ram.

shell A shell is a hard covering. Some animals have shells. Some eggs have shells. Some seeds have shells.

Oscar, look at my collection of sea**shells.**
I have a **shell** collection, too, Betty Lou—egg**shells**!

shine When something shines, it makes a bright light. Something can also shine if light bounces off it.

Marshal Grover's badge **shines** because it is so clean.

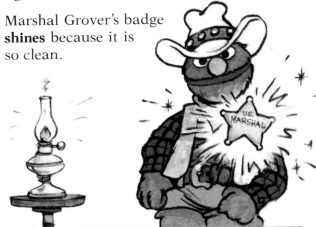

ship A ship is a large boat. Some ships have sails and some have engines. Some have both.

Captain Bert's **ship** is sailing into the harbor.

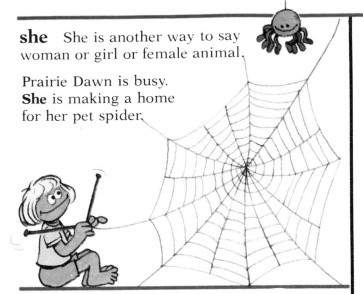

shirt A shirt is a piece of clothing you wear on the top part of your body.

shoe A shoe is something you wear on your foot.

Ernie is wearing a striped **shirt** and one saddle **shoe.**

shop A shop is a store where you can buy things.

Cookie Monster loves to go **shopping** at the cookie **shop.**

short Something that is short is not as high as something that is tall.

When something is short, the beginning is close to the end.

Big Bird is tall.
Little Bird is **short.**
Little Bird's jump rope is too **short** for Big Bird.

shoulder Your shoulder is a part of your body. Your arms are attached to your shoulders. Look up the word body.

The Count's pet bat is sitting on his **shoulder.**

shout When you shout, you call out loudly.

MUD! FRESH MUD! GET YOUR MUD HERE!
I love to hear the Mudman **shout.**
FRESH MUD

shovel A shovel is a tool used to scoop things up.

Farmer Grover is using his snow **shovel** to **shovel** snow.

show When you show something, you put it where it can be seen.

Let me **show** you my seashell collection.
Let me **show** you my nutshell collection.

show A show is something special to be seen or heard. A show can be a movie, a play, or a program on radio or television.

Grover Knover is putting on a **show.** Everyone is watching.

shut When you shut something, you close it.

I must **shut** the barn door so the cows will not get out.

sick When you are sick, you are not healthy.

Biff is **sick.** He has a cold.

Get Well Soon— Sully

side The side of something is the part that is not the top, bottom, front, or back.

Herry Monster is lifting a chest. There are two handles— one on each **side.**

Side can also mean the team you are on.
Hurray for our **side**!

sign A sign tells you something. A printed sign uses words or pictures. You can also make signs with your hands in special ways.

What do these **signs** tell you?

STOP
When you **sign** your name, you write your name.

silent Silent means without any sound.

silly When something is silly, it does not make sense and may be funny.

Isn't Marshal Grover **silly**?

sing When you sing, you make music with your voice.

Bert likes to **sing** to Bernice. Bernice thinks he is a good **singer.**

single Single is a word that means one.

sink A sink is a bowl that can be filled with water and has a drain to let the water out.

Cookie the baker has a **sink** full of dirty dishes.

sink When something sinks, it goes down. In water, some things float and some things sink.

Grover's rowboat is beginning to **sink.**

sister If your mother and father have another child who is a girl, she is your sister.

sit When you sit, you rest on the lower part of your body. Your weight is off your feet.

Why did the monster **sit** on the clock?
He wanted to be on time!
crunch!

six Six is a number. Six is one more than five.

sixteen Sixteen is a number. Sixteen is ten plus six more.

Oscar has ten red apple cores and **six** green apple cores. He has **sixteen** apple cores all together.

size The size of something is how big or how small it is.

Figgy Fizz comes in three different **sizes**—small, medium, and large.

skate A skate is something you wear on your foot to help you move on ice, hard floors, or sidewalks. Some skates have runners and some have wheels.

Betty Lou wears roller **skates** to **skate** on the sidewalk.

Farley wears ice **skates** to **skate** on the ice.

skeleton Your skeleton is all the bones of your body fitted together. All people and most animals have skeletons. Look up the word bone.

This is a picture of a human **skeleton.**
This is a picture of a dinosaur **skeleton.**

skin Your skin is the outer covering of your body. Animals and fruits and vegetables also have skins.

My pet snake, Sammy, has pretty stripes on his **skin.**
I do not have stripes on my **skin.**

skip When you skip, you take little hops while you run.

I like to walk.
I like to **skip.**

When you **skip** something, you leave it out.
I read the whole dictionary and didn't **skip** one word.

skirt A skirt is a piece of clothing. It hangs from your waist.

Rodeo Rosie is wearing a brown **skirt.**

sled A sled is something with runners that slides on the snow or the ice.

Betty Lou is coasting down the hill on her **sled.**

sky The sky is the covering of air and clouds over the world.

I love to fly my little airplane in the **sky.**

sleep When you sleep, you close your eyes and rest your whole body.

Grover likes to **sleep** with his teddy bear.

slide Slide means to move smoothly across a surface.

slide A slide is a playground toy. After you climb to the top, you slide to the bottom.

Big Bird likes to **slide** down the **slide.**

slip When you slip, you slide and start to fall.

slippery Something that is slippery can make you slip.

OOOOPS!

Banana peels are **slippery.** If you step on one, you may **slip.**

slow Slow means not fast.

Barkley is watching a snail race.
Snails are **slow.**

woof!
1
2
3
4

small Small means little.

Big Bird has a large mailbox.

Little Bird has a **small** mailbox.

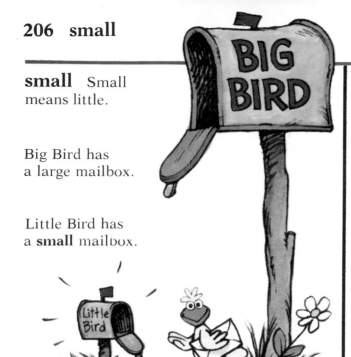

smell When you smell something, you breathe an odor in through your nose.

smile When you smile, the corners of your mouth turn up and you look happy.

Rubber Duckie makes Ernie **smile.**

smoke Smoke is the cloud that rises from something burning.

Prairie Dawn's campfire is still burning. She can see the **smoke.**

smooth Something that is smooth has a surface that is not rough or wrinkled or bumpy.

sneeze When you sneeze, air comes out of your nose and mouth and you make a loud sound like AH-CHOO.

snow Snow is tiny white flakes of frozen water that fall from the clouds.

so So means very.

I love the **snow**— **so, so** much.

soap Soap is something used with water to clean things.

Ernie is cleaning Rubber Duckie with **soap.**

sock A sock is something made of cloth that you wear on your foot. You put on your sock before you put on your shoe.

There is a hole in the Count's **sock.**

1 ... one hole! Wonderful!

soft When something is soft, it is not hard or stiff.

Three of these things belong together. One of these things is not the same.

A teddy bear, a pillow, and a blanket are all **soft** things. A lunchbox is a hard thing. The lunchbox does not belong.

son If a father and mother have a child who is a boy, that child is their son.

They are my parents.
He is our **son.**

song A song is something to sing.

soon Soon is a word that means not too long from now.

Doin' the Pigeon ... doin' the Pigeon ...
When will this **song** be over?
Soon.

sorry When you are sorry, you are sad about something that has happened.

I'm **sorry** I broke your toy airplane, Farley. I'll try to fix it.

sound A sound is something you hear.

Hey, Oscar! What was that terrible **sound** I heard a moment ago?
I didn't hear anything, Betty Lou. I was too busy playing my trombone.

soup Soup is a liquid food made by cooking meat, vegetables, or fruits in water.

Hey, waiter! There's a fly in my **soup.**
Don't worry, sir. Flies don't eat much.

speak When you speak, you talk.

I will now **speak** about my favorite subject—pigeons.
Happiness is...
In the beginning...
PIGEON Lovers' CLUB

special Special is a word that means not like all the others.

Mr. Snuffle-upagus is my **special** friend.

speed The speed of something is how fast it goes.

Grover Knover can move with great **speed.**

spell When you spell a word, you say or write its letters in the right order.

Oscar can **spell** SCRAM.

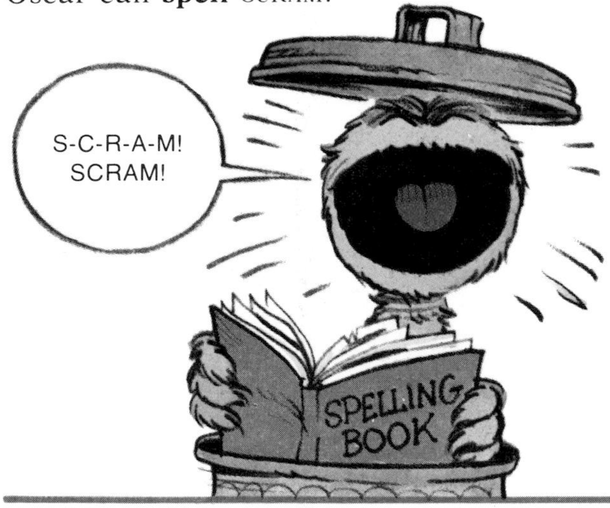
S-C-R-A-M!
SCRAM!
SPELLING BOOK

spider A spider is a very small animal with eight legs. Many spiders spin webs to catch insects for food.

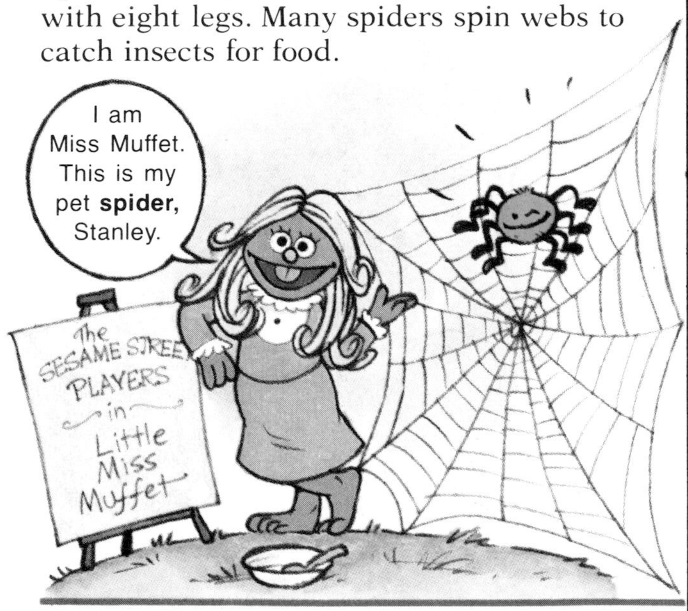
I am Miss Muffet. This is my pet **spider,** Stanley.
The SESAME STREET PLAYERS in Little Miss Muffet

spill When something spills, it falls out of a container—usually by mistake.

Farley did not want to **spill** his jellybeans. But he did.

Jelly-beans

spin When you spin something, you turn it around and around quickly.
When something spins, it turns around quickly.

Ernie likes to **spin** his top.
His top is **spinning** fast.

spoon A spoon is a tool used to stir or scoop up food. You sometimes use a spoon when you eat.

Bert eats his oatmeal with a **spoon.**

spot A spot is a kind of mark.

Look! There is a **spot** on my cape. Let me count it. 1 ... one **spot**! Wonderful!

spread When you spread something, you smooth it out so that it covers more space.

Bert likes to **spread** peanut butter on a piece of bread.

PEANUT BUTTER

spring Spring is the name of a season. Spring comes after winter.

The leaves on the trees are beginning to grow. It must be **spring**.

stage A stage is the place in the theater where the actors act, the dancers dance, and the singers sing.

Big Bird is acting on the **stage.**

square A square is a shape with four corners and four sides of the same length.

One of these shapes is not like the others. One of these shapes does not belong.

The circle does not have four corners and four sides. It is not a **square.** It does not belong.

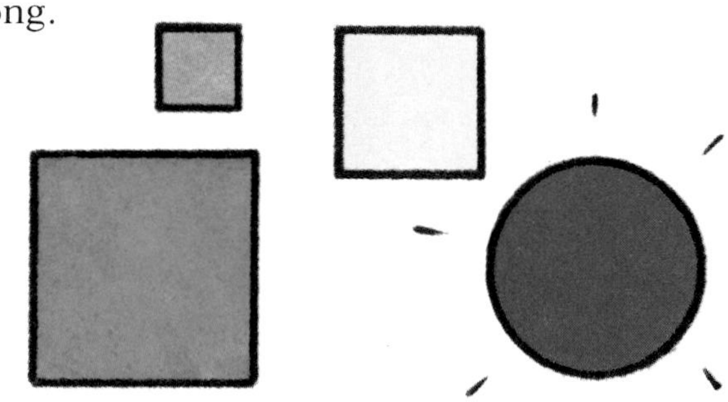

stairs Stairs are a set of steps. You can go up stairs and you can go down stairs.

stamp A stamp is a small piece of paper that you put on a letter or package to show that you have paid to send it.

squeeze When you squeeze something, you press it.

Ernie has to **squeeze** the sponge to get the water out.

stand When you stand, you are on your feet, but your feet are not moving.

Farley has to **stand** in line to buy a **stamp** for his letter.

star A star is another sun—far, far away. At night a star looks like a tiny point of light in the sky.

Grover the astronaut can see many **stars.**

star A star is also a shape.

Grover's spaceship has a **star** on its side.

A **star** is also a famous person in a show.
clap
clap clap
HURRAY!
clap
YEA!

stay When you stay, you do not leave.

Connie the witch is going on a trip. The other witches will **stay** at home.

steal When someone steals, that person takes something that does not belong to him or her.

Watch out for the Cookie Thief! He might **steal** your cookies.
WANTED The Great COOKIE THIEF
COOKIES

start When you start something, you begin it or get it going.

Grouches, **start** your grouchmobiles so I can **start** the race.
STARTER
START

step A step is what you put your foot on when you go up or down stairs.

The stairs in my castle have five hundred and sixty-eight **steps.** I love to count them all. 1 ... one **step** ... 2 ...two **steps** ...

stick A stick is a long, thin piece of wood.

Barkley likes to play with a **stick.**

stick When you make something stick, it stays where you put it.

GLUE
How do you like my latest work of art? I used glue to make all these pieces of garbage **stick** to my hat.

still Still means not moving or not talking.

stone A stone is a rock. Some things are made out of stone.

Farmer Grover is lifting a heavy **stone.**

stop When something stops, it does not keep going.

Grover Knover has to **stop** at the **stop** sign.

store A store is a place where you can buy things.

Grover's mother bought a new book at the book**store.**

story A story is something to tell. Stories can be true or imaginary. You can tell a story out loud or write it.

stove A stove is a thing used for cooking or heating.

Grover's mother is reading the **story** of Goldilocks and the three bears.

Papa Bear was cooking porridge on the **stove.**

straight Straight means without a bend or a curve or a curl or a twist.

This is a **straight** line. The other lines are not **straight.**
straight line

curly line
curved line

strange Strange means odd, unusual, or not seen or heard before.

There is a **strange** bird in Big Bird's nest.

A **stranger** is someone you don't know.
Hi. My name is Fred.
BUS STOP

street A street is a road in a town or a city. A street usually has buildings on it.

Sesame **Street** is a nice **street** to live on.

stretch When you stretch something, you make it longer or bigger.

Don't put my sweater on, Herry. You will **stretch** it.

string A string is a very thin rope.

Big Bird is tying a package with **string.**

strong Strong means having lots of power or not easily broken.

Herry can lift heavy barbells. Herry is **strong.**

The third little pig's house was **strong.** The wolf could not blow it down.

subtract When you subtract, you take something away.

If I **subtract** one apple from four apples, I will have three apples.
4
-1
3

subway A subway is an underground railroad. Some cities have subways.

Biff rides to work on the **subway.**

suddenly Suddenly means all at once.

The Monster Marching Band had to stop **suddenly.**

sugar Sugar is something you can put in food to make it taste sweeter.

This lemonade tastes too sweet. There is too much **sugar** in it.
SUGAR

summer Summer is the name of a season. Summer comes after spring.

sun The sun is a star. It gives light and warmth and energy to all living things on the earth.

The **sun** is the brightest light in the sky.

The days are getting longer and hotter. It must be **summer.**

super Super means extra-big, extra-strong, extra-smart, or extra-good.

I, **Super** Grover, am proud that I can help people with my **super** powers.
SUPER AWARD FOR SUPER GROVER

sure When you are sure about something, you know that it is true. You are certain.

surprise A surprise is something you do not know about or expect.

TELEPHONE
I am **sure** I saw Grover Monster go into that phone booth.

TELEPHONE
Super Grover! What a **surprise** to see you!

swallow When you swallow food or water, it goes down your throat to your stomach.

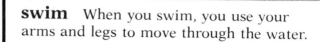

Sammy the snake will now **swallow** another apple.

sweep To sweep means to brush away. You can use a broom to sweep dirt.

This is the way I **sweep** my nest, **sweep** my nest, **sweep** my nest....

sweet When something is sweet, it is nice to taste or smell or hear or see. When something tastes sweet, it usually has sugar in it.

How **sweet**!
sniff!
How **sweet**!

Tweet
Tweet
Tweet
How **sweet**!
How **sweet**!

swim When you swim, you use your arms and legs to move through the water.

Prairie Dawn likes to **swim**.
She is a good **swimmer**.

swing A swing is a hanging seat that moves back and forth.

What time is it when Herry Monster sits on your **swing**?
Time to get a new **swing**.

Just think of all the super words that begin with S— scummy, slimy, sloppy, soggy, stinky, swampy— and my special favorite— SCRAM!

table A table is a piece of furniture with a flat top and legs.

Lay your cards on the **table,** Rosie!

tail A tail is a part of an animal's body. Some animals have tails and some animals do not.

Different animals have different kinds of **tails.**

I'm an animal, but I don't have a **tail.**

take When you take something, you catch hold of it, or have it with you when you go somewhere. Take also means do or make.

Oh, Mommy, I am so scared of the dark.

Don't be frightened, Grover, dear. **Take** my hand and I will **take** you home. Then you can **take** your bath.

talk When you talk, you say words.

Biff likes to **talk.** Sully likes to listen.

Hey, Sully, what do you have in your lunchbox? I have a peanut butter sandwich. I love peanut butter....

tall Something tall is long from top to bottom. It is not short. The height of something is how tall it is.

taste When you taste something, you find out what flavor it has. You taste things with your tongue.

I can taste this lemon. It is sour.
I can taste this lollipop. It is sweet.

taxi A taxi is a special kind of car. You pay a taxi driver to drive you somewhere.

Bert and Ernie are going on a trip. They are taking a **taxi** to the airport.

teach When you teach, you help someone to learn.

teacher A teacher is someone who teaches—usually at a school.

Grover's **teacher** is trying to **teach** him how to write his name.

team A team is a group of people who work together to do the same thing.

tear A tear is a tiny drop of water that comes from your eye when you cry.

Farley has **tears** in his eyes. He is crying because he dropped his apple in the sandbox.

tear When you tear something, you pull it apart.

I like to **tear** paper because **torn** paper is one of my favorite kinds of trash.

rrrrip!

telephone A telephone is used to send or receive sounds. When you use a telephone, you can talk to someone who is far away.

Big Bird is talking to Granny Bird on the **telephone.**

Gee, Granny. I sure like the birdseed cookies you sent to me.

I sure like the picture you sent to *me*, Big Bird.

television A television is a machine. When you turn on a television, you can see people and things and hear the sounds they make.

Bert is watching his favorite show on **television.**

tell When you tell something, you put it into words.

temperature The temperature of something is how hot or how cold it is. You use a thermometer to measure temperature.

Grover has a thermometer in his mouth. His mother is taking his **temperature.**

Don't feel bad, Grover, dear. I will **tell** you a story.

ten Ten is a number. Ten is one more than nine.

I have **ten** bats in my belfry.

thank When you thank someone, you say you like what that person did for you.

Gee, Barkley, I want to **thank** you for finding my other shoe.

that That means which or the one there.

LET'S MAKE A CHOICE!
Hi, folks! It's time to play— LET'S MAKE A CHOICE! Today's contestant is Betty Lou. Betty Lou, what's your choice— this or **that**?
I choose **that.**
THIS
THAT

Let's see what's inside the package **that** Betty Lou chose. It's ...
a year's supply of trash from Oscar the Grouch! Better luck next time, Betty Lou!
THIS
THAT

If you want to see Betty Lou play this game again, look up the words these, this, and those.

the The means a certain one.

Bert, have you seen Rubber Duckie?
Do you mean **the** rubber duckie that I found in my paper clip collection, Ernie?

theater A theater is a place where you can see a play or a movie or another kind of show.

The Count is arriving at the **theater.**

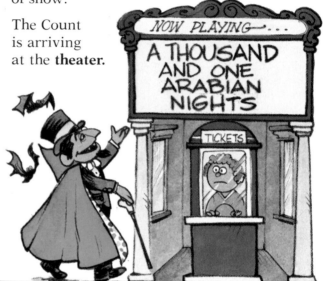

their Their is another way of saying belonging to them. When something is theirs, it belongs to them.

them Them is another way of saying the ones I am talking about.

The Busbys are sitting on **their** bicycle.

This bicycle is mine. That bicycle is **theirs.** It belongs to **them.**

then Then means at that time.

A long time ago there was a little girl named Miss Muffet who was sitting on a tuffet eating her curds and whey.
Then what happened?
Little Miss Muffet
Well, along came a spider who sat down beside her.
Then what happened?
Little Miss Muffet shared her curds and whey with the spider.

there There means in that place.

Where shall I put this mud, Oscar?
MUDMAN DELIVERY
Over there, in my mud box.
OSCAR'S MUDBOX

these These means the ones here.

they They means the people or things I am talking about.

LET'S MAKE A CHOICE!
Well, Betty Lou, are you ready to play LET'S MAKE A CHOICE? Here is today's choice. . . . What do you choose, Betty Lou— these or those?
I choose these.
THOSE
THESE
Then let's see what's inside these packages. Betty Lou, you chose . . .
a year's supply of sardine-and-sour-pickle sandwiches from Oscar the Grouch!
I don't like sardine-and-sour-pickle sandwiches. They make me sick.
THESE

thick When something solid is thick, it is big from side to side. When something liquid is thick, it is gooey and hard to pour.

thin When something is thin, it is not thick.

thing A thing can be seen or heard or touched or smelled. A thing can also be done or said or thought of.

*Hand me that **thick** board, Sully. This board is too **thin**.*

*This paint is too **thick**.*

*This paint is too **thin**.*

*By the way, what is this **thing** we're building?*

think When you think, you use your mind.

*Hey, Bert. Does this beach umbrella make you **think** of building sand castles?*

*No, Ernie. It makes me **think** of vacuuming the rug. That beach umbrella was full of sand before you opened it.*

thirsty When you are thirsty, you want something to drink.

Marshal Grover and Fred are **thirsty.**

Here you are— two big glasses of milk!

thirteen Thirteen is a number. Thirteen is ten plus three more.

Bert has three big boxes of oatmeal and ten small boxes of oatmeal. He has **thirteen** boxes of oatmeal all together.

OAT-MEAL *Large*

OAT-MEAL *Large*

OAT-MEAL *Large*

13

OAT-MEAL

OAT-MEAL

OAT-MEAL

OAT-MEAL

OAT-MEAL

OAT-MEAL

OAT-MEAL

OAT-MEAL

OAT-MEAL

OAT-MEAL

this This means the one here.

those Those means the ones there.

LET'S MAKE A CHOICE!

Here's our contestant, Betty Lou, back to play— LET'S MAKE A CHOICE! Once more, Betty Lou . . . what do you choose— **this** or that or these or **those**?
This or that? These or **those**? **Those** or these? **This** or that? AARRRGGGHH! I can't stand it. Nothing! I choose nothing!
THAT
THOSE
THIS
THESE

Then let's see what you did not choose. In **this** package we find— a little puppy! In that package we find—a large bag of jellybeans! In these packages we find— cute, adorable kittens! And in **those** packages—a year's supply of coconut cream pies! I'm sorry, Betty Lou. And thanks for being such a wonderful contestant.
THOSE
THAT
THIS
THESE

If you want to see what Betty Lou is thinking, look up the word thought.

thought A thought is an idea. A thought is what someone thinks.

Betty Lou's **thought:**

thread A thread is a thin piece of string used for sewing.

three Three is a number. Three is one more than two.

Farley is sewing **three** buttons on his shirt with **thread.**

through Through means from one side to the other side or from one end to the other end of something.

Barkley can jump **through** a hoop.

Are you **through** with that dictionary? I need it.

throw When you throw something, you toss it through the air.

When I **throw** the stick, Barkley runs after it.

thumb Your thumb is one of the fingers on your hand. Look up the word hand.

Ernie, why do you have a string tied around your **thumb**?
So I won't forget to buy more string.

thunder Thunder is the loud noise you sometimes hear when there is lightning. Look up the word lightning.

KA-BOOM!
Ahh. One lovely bolt of lightning and one fabulous clap of **thunder**! Wonderful!

ticket A ticket is a piece of paper that allows you to do something. Sometimes you pay money for a ticket.

tickle When something tickles you, it touches you lightly and makes you laugh.

Big Bird is riding on the train. The conductor is taking his **ticket.**

Feathers can **tickle.**
Hee hee hee ho ho ho ha ha ha ha hoo hoo hoo

tie When you tie a string, rope, or ribbon, you put a knot or bow in it.

Ernie can **tie** his shoelaces.

A **tie** is something you can wear around your neck.

tiger A tiger is a big, wild orange cat with black stripes.

I've always wondered if a **tiger** is orange with black stripes, or black with orange stripes.
ROAR!
I don't think I'll wait to find out.

tight When something is tight, it fits too closely. It is not loose.

My Uncle Charlie knitted this nice sweater for me. But he must not know how much I've grown. Look how **tight** it is.

time Time is when something happens. Time is measured in seconds, minutes, hours, days, weeks, months, and years.

What **time** is it, Ernie?
It's six o'clock, Bert.
Oh, good! It's **time** for the Pigeon News.
If you have a good **time,** you enjoy yourself. If you have a good **time,** you enjoy yourself.
He said that two **times.**

tired When you are tired, you need to rest.

YAWN!
Oh, dear. I am **tired.** I think I will go home to take my nap.

to To means in the direction of.

Betty Lou is throwing a ball **to** Barkley.

today Today is the day it is now.

Today is my birthday. **Today** everyone does everything just the way I like it. No cake, no presents, and nobody saying HAPPY BIRTHDAY.

toe Your toe is a part of your foot. You have five toes on each foot. Look up the word body.

Bert is doing his exercises.
He is touching his **toes.**

together Together means with each other.

tomato A tomato is a round red fruit that grows on vines above the ground.

~Tomato~

Hi, Oscar! We are all here **together** because it's your birthday today.

Here is a cake made out of mud.

And here's a present from all of us.

Wow! It's a rotten **tomato.** It's just what I wanted. Gee, thanks, everyone, for such a perfect birthday.

Have a Rotten Birthday

tomorrow Tomorrow is the day that comes after today.

I can't wait until **tomorrow.** Granny Bird just said she is coming to visit.

click

tongue Your tongue is a part of your mouth. It helps you speak and taste.

Barkley likes to taste ice cream with his **tongue.**

tonight Tonight is the night of the day that it is now.

Tonight I can see stars in the sky. That is the Big Dipper.

too Too means also.

What is blue and furry and lovable and has eight wheels?

Grover on roller skates!

And I am *cute,* **too.**

too Too can also mean more than enough.

tool A tool is used to do work. Here are some different kinds of tools.

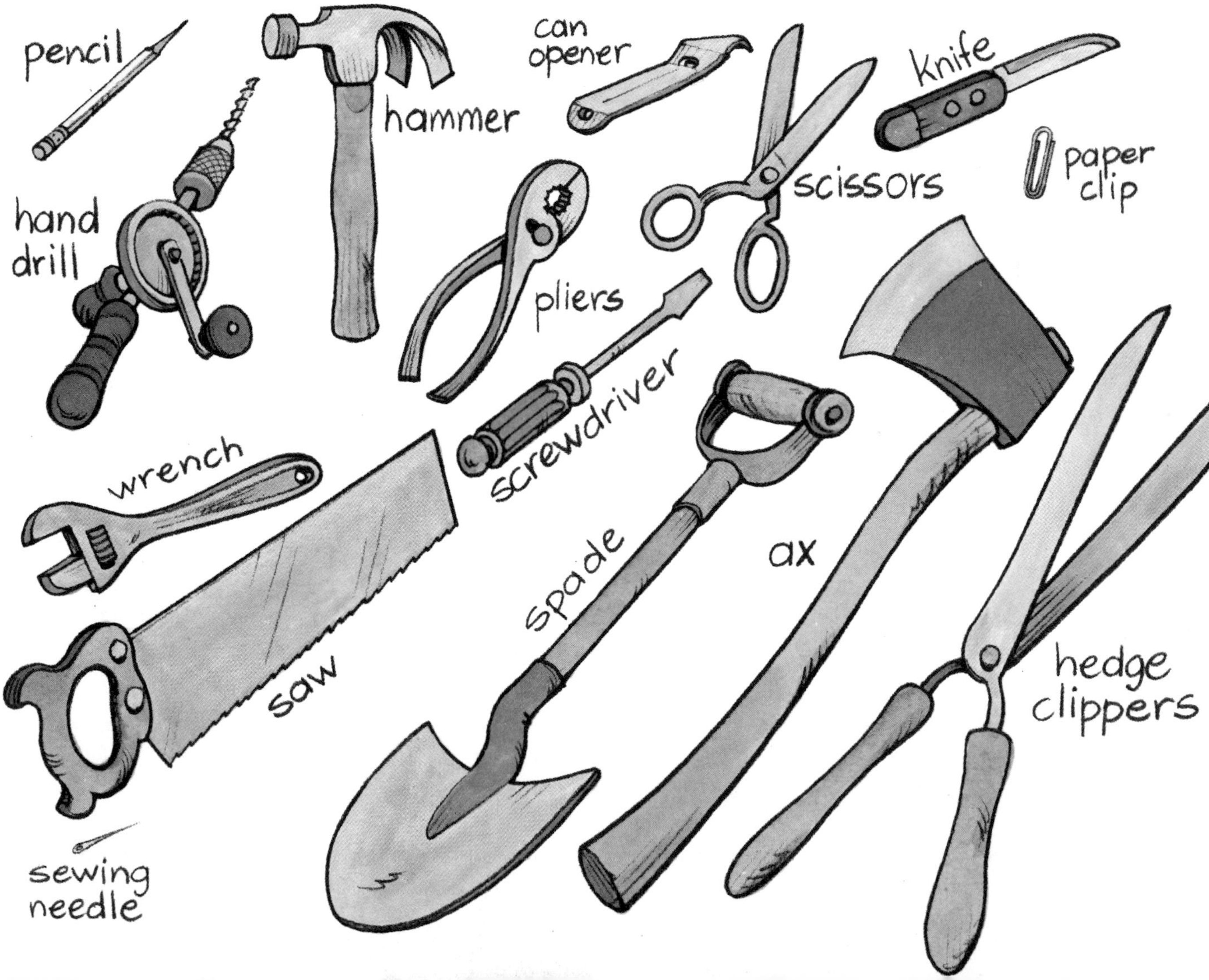
pencil
hammer
can opener
knife
hand drill
pliers
scissors
paper clip
screwdriver
wrench
saw
spade
ax
hedge clippers
sewing needle

tooth A tooth is one of your teeth. Teeth are in your mouth and are used for biting and chewing.

Frazzle is brushing his **teeth.** He has one **tooth**brush for each **tooth.**

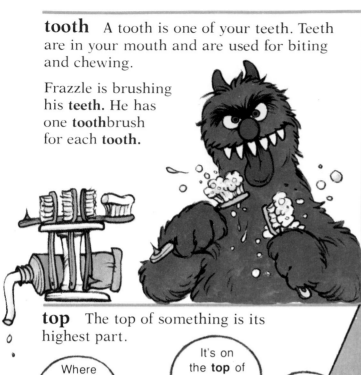

top The top of something is its highest part.

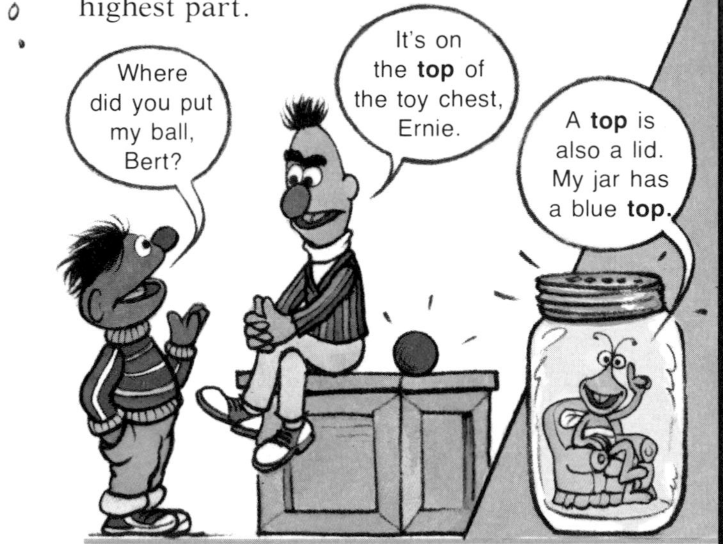
Where did you put my ball, Bert?
It's on the **top** of the toy chest, Ernie.
A **top** is also a lid. My jar has a blue **top.**

touch When you touch something, you feel it with your hand or another part of your body.

I love to **touch** my little lamb. He feels so soft.

towel A towel is a piece of cloth or paper that is used for drying something wet.

Herry Monster took a shower. He is drying himself with a **towel.**

town A town is a place where many people live and work. A town is usually smaller than a city.

Marshal Grover is riding into **town.**

toy A toy is something to play with.

Three of these things belong together. One of these things is not the same.

Rubber Duckie, a toy airplane, and a jack-in-the box are all **toys.** Bert's shoe is something to wear. Bert's shoe does not belong.

train A train is a string of railroad cars pulled along a track by an engine.

The cars have to stop so the **train** can go by.

trash Trash is things that are thrown away.

travel When you travel, you go from one place to another.

Whenever I **travel,** I collect **trash** on the way.
ROAD CLOSED

tree A tree is a tall plant with a woody stem called a trunk. A tree has branches and leaves or needles.

Who is hiding behind each **tree**?

triangle A triangle is a shape with three sides and three corners.

Three of these things belong together.
One of these things is not the same.
The square has four sides and four corners.
The square does not belong.

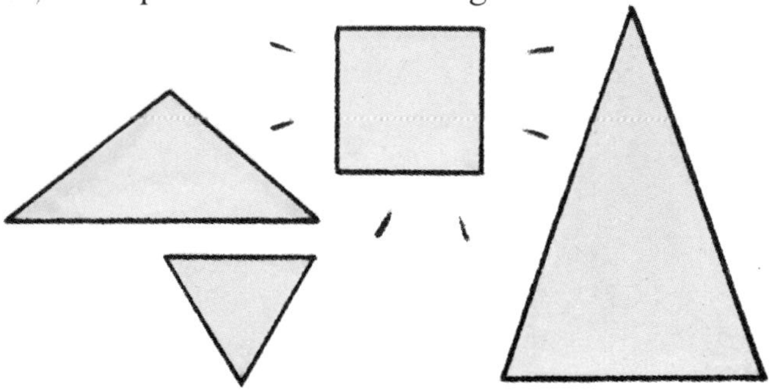

trick A trick is a clever thing you can do.

The Amazing Mumford
is doing a magic **trick.**

tricycle A tricycle is something to ride. It has three wheels, a seat, handlebars, and pedals.

Barkley can ride a **tricycle.**

That is a good trick for a dog!

trip When you go on a trip, you travel somewhere.

Farley is going on a **trip.**
He is taking the train.

Have a nice **trip,** Farley.

trip When you trip, your foot bumps into something and you stumble or fall.

Grover, dear, be careful not to **trip** on the roller skate.
Oooops! You **tripped.**

trouble When you are having trouble, you are having a problem.

Hey, Bert! I'm having **trouble** moving this box. What's in it?
Ernie, that's where I keep my rock collection.

truck A truck is a machine with an engine and four or more wheels. It is used to carry loads or do other kinds of work.

I just love to count **trucks.**

true When something is true, it is real. It is not false or a lie.

Is it **true** that a whale is the largest animal?
It's **true.**

trunk A trunk is a big suitcase.

trunk A trunk is also an elephant's nose.

trunk A trunk can also be the woody stem of a tree.

I, the Amazing Mumford, will now pull from this perfectly empty **trunk** two other **trunks.**
A LA PEANUT BUTTER SANDWICHES!

1, 2, 3... three **trunks**! Amazing!

try When you try to do something, you make an effort to do it.

I, Grover Knover, will **try** to jump over this pond.
Nice **try,** Grover Knover!
Try again.

turn When something turns, it goes around and around or changes direction.

When I ride my bicycle, the wheels **turn** very fast.
When I **turn** a corner, I change direction.

turn When one thing turns into another thing, it becomes something else.

When water freezes, it **turns** into ice.
ice cubes
water

turtle A turtle is an animal with a hard shell and a soft body. A turtle can pull its head and arms and legs inside its shell.

Some people say that **turtles** can hide inside their shells and look just like rocks. Do you believe that?
Oh!

twelve Twelve is a number. Twelve is ten plus two more.

Bert has ten blue shoelaces and two orange shoelaces. Bert has **twelve** shoelaces all together.

12
Twelve things make a dozen.

twenty Twenty is a number. Twenty is ten plus ten more.

Ernie has ten red jellybeans and ten green jellybeans. Ernie has **twenty** jellybeans all together.

twin A twin is one of two children who have the same mother and father and are born at the same time. Some twins look exactly alike. Some twins do not look like each other.

The Busby **twins** look alike.

The Henderson **twins** do not look alike.

two Two is a number. Two is one more than one.

There are **two** Busby twins.

This dictionary is not as terrible as I thought. The T section has rotten tomatoes, garbage trucks, and trash, trash, trash!

Uu

A B C D E F G H I J K L M N O P Q R S T **U** V W X Y Z

ugly When you think something is ugly, you do not like to look at it or hear it.

Oscar, please clean up this **ugly** pile of trash.
Ugly? I think it's beautiful.

umbrella An umbrella is a folding cover that protects you from the rain or the sun.

When can three big monsters fit under a tiny **umbrella** and not get wet?
When it is not raining.
RRRR!

uncle Your uncle is the brother of your mother or your father. Your aunt's husband is also your uncle.

Uncle Bob
Uncle Bob is my mother's brother. **Uncle** Lew is my father's brother.
Uncle Lew
Mother
Father
Me

under Under means below.

Super Grover is flying **under** the bridge. Little Bird is flying over the bridge.

understand When you understand something, you know what it means.

underwear The clothes you wear under your other clothes are called underwear. Undershirts and underpants are two kinds of underwear.

There are stars on the Amazing Mumford's **underwear.**

undress When you undress, you take off your clothes.

Ernie must **undress** before he can take a bath.

unhappy When you are unhappy, you do not feel happy—you feel sad.

Bert is **unhappy.** He lost his whole bottle cap collection.

until Until means up to the time of.

Farmer Grover always waits at the gate **until** the cows come home.

unusual Unusual means not usual. Something that is unusual is something that you are not used to seeing or hearing or feeling.

up When you go up, you move to a higher place.

upside down When something is upside down, the top is on the bottom and the bottom is on the top.

Big Bird is **upside down.**

us Us is another way of saying you and me.

use When you use a thing, you do something with it.

usual Something that is usual is something that you are used to seeing, hearing, or feeling.

Bert is having his **usual** breakfast.

usually Usually means most often or in the ordinary way.

vacation A vacation is a special time when someone does not work or go to school.

Guy Smiley is on **vacation.**

vacuum When you vacuum, you use a vacuum cleaner to suck up dust and dirt.

Bert likes to **vacuum** the rug.

valentine A valentine is a card that you send on Valentine's Day to someone you like.

Big Bird sent Snuffle-upagus a **valentine** on the fourteenth of February.

vase A vase is a container used for holding flowers.

Mr. Snuffle-upagus sent me a flower for Valentine's Day.

Big Bird put his flower in a **vase.**

vegetable A vegetable is a plant that is used for food.

Farmer Grover is picking **vegetables** in his **vegetable** garden.

vehicle A vehicle is something that can carry people or things from one place to another. Wagons, automobiles, trucks, and sleds are different kinds of vehicles.

I love to count **vehicles.**
R.R.
123

very Very means more than usual or much.

My dog is big, but Barkley is **very** big.

village A village is a small town.

When the Count was born, his parents announced the news to all the people who lived in the **village.**

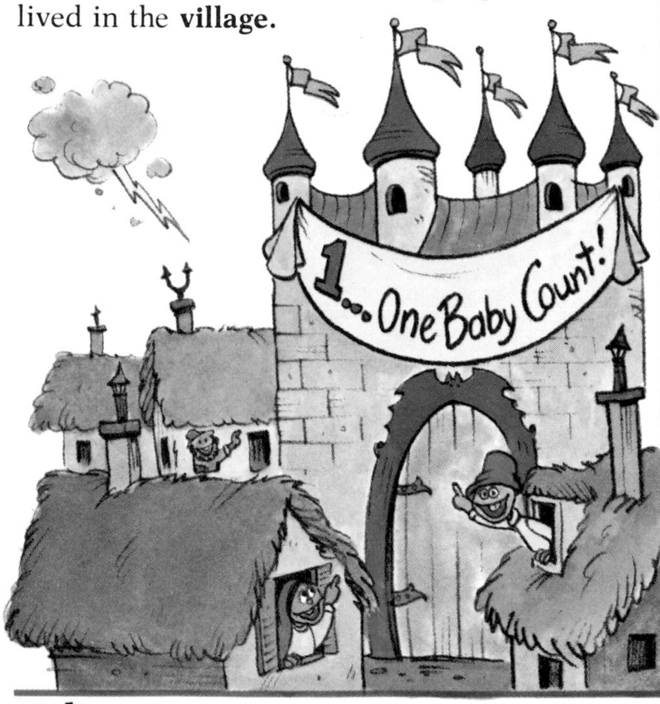
1... One Baby Count!

violin A violin is a musical instrument. It has four strings and is played with a bow. Look up the word bow.

The Count loves to play the **violin.**

visit When you visit, you go to see someone or something.

Prairie Dawn likes to **visit** the museum.

DON'T TOUCH!

voice Your voice is the sound you make while talking or shouting or singing.

Hello, Bird!
I can hear Mr. Snuffle-upagus' **voice.**

Vacation is a word that begins with V. I would be very glad to take a vacation from this dictionary.

Ww

A B C D E F G H I J K L M N O P Q R S T U V W X Y Z

wagon A wagon is used to carry things. A wagon has four wheels and is usually pulled.

wait When you wait, you stop what you are doing or stay where you are until something happens.

Fred has to **wait** for Farmer Grover to load the **wagon.**

YAWN!

waiter A waiter is a person who takes orders and serves food in a restaurant.

Waiter! What is this fly doing in my soup?
He is doing the backstroke, sir.

Grover the **waiter** is serving alphabet soup.

wake When you wake, you stop sleeping.

ZZZZ
Wake up, Ernie! The Late Pigeon News is over. It's time to go to bed.

walk When you walk, you move by taking steps.

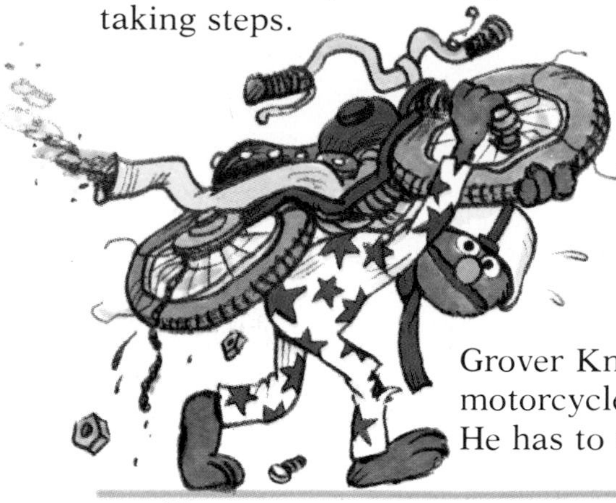

Grover Knover's motorcycle is broken. He has to **walk.**

wall A wall is the side of a building or a room. A wall can also be a kind of fence.

Biff and Sully are painting the **walls** of the room blue.

Oscar is building a **wall** around his trash can.

I **want** a **wall** around my trash can so people won't bother me.

want When you want something, you would like to have it.

warm When something is warm, it is more hot than cold. But it is not *very* hot.

The water in the bathtub is **warm**— just right for Rubber Duckie and me.

was Ernie **was** dirty. Now he is clean.

wash When you wash something, you clean it with water and sometimes soap.

Betty Lou likes to **wash** Barkley. Barkley does not like to be **washed.**

waste When you waste something, you do not make good use of it.

This oatmeal box is just what I need to make a drum. I'll just get rid of all this oatmeal . . . .
Don't **waste** that oatmeal! I'll use it to make oatmeal bread.
OAT-MEAL

watch A watch is a small clock that you can wear on your wrist or carry in your pocket. A watch shows you what time it is.

Bert has a **watch** on his wrist.

watch When you watch something, you look at it.

Bert likes to **watch** the sun rise.

Today the sun is rising at six o'clock.

water Water is wet. We use water to drink, to cook with, and to clean with. All living things need water.

Herry Monster is taking a bath in hot **water.** He is drinking a glass of cold **water.**

way The way you do something is how you do it.

This is the **way** Ernie makes his bed.

This is the **way** Bert makes his bed.

way The way you go is the direction or path in which you move.

we We is another way of saying you and I.

We are going this **way.** They are going that **way.**

weak Something that is weak breaks easily or is not strong.

The toy wagon is **weak.** It will not hold Barkley.

wear When you wear something, you have it on your body.

Marshal Grover **wears** a hat, a vest, chaps, and a shiny badge.

weather Weather can be sunny, cloudy, rainy, windy, or snowy. The weather is also how hot or how cold it is outside.

The mail carrier has to deliver the mail in all kinds of **weather.**

Through rain or snow or sleet or hail, I see that Sesame Gulch gets the mail.
U.S. MAIL

week A week is seven days long. Each day in the week has a special name. Look up the word calendar.

Bert has a busy **week.**

SUNDAY—Take Bernice for a walk.
MONDAY—Work on my bottle cap collection.
TUESDAY—Work on my paper clip collection.
WEDNESDAY—Buy oatmeal.
THURSDAY—Clean closet.
FRIDAY—Go To Pigeon Lovers' meeting.
SATURDAY—Polish saddle shoes.

weigh When you weigh something, you find out how heavy it is.

weight The weight of something is how heavy it is. Your weight is how heavy you are.

Stand still, Farley. I want to **weigh** you. This scale will tell me your **weight.**

well When you are well, you are not sick. You are healthy.

Farley is **well.**

You are very healthy, Farley.
When you do something **well,** you do it in a good way.
I roller skate **well.**

were The Busby twins **were** at the zoo.

We **were** both at the zoo yesterday.
You **were** there, too.

wet When something is wet, it has water or another liquid on it. It is not dry.

Barkley is **wet.**

Now everyone is **wet.**

whale A whale is a huge animal that lives in the ocean and looks like a fish. But it is not a fish. A whale breathes air.

AQUARIUM
The dictionary says that a **whale** looks like a fish but is not a fish.

what What is a word used to ask questions or talk about people and things.

What are you holding behind your back?
I have **what** my mother gave me for lunch.

wheel A wheel is something that is shaped like a circle and can roll or turn.

Three of these things belong together.
One of these things is not the same.

The wagon, the tricycle, and the roller skates are all things that have **wheels.**
The sled does not have **wheels.**
The sled does not belong.

when When is a word used to ask questions or talk about time.

When does Cookie Monster *not* want a cookie?
When he wants *two* cookies!

where Where is a word used to ask questions or talk about places.

which Which is a word used to ask questions or talk about people or things.

while While means during the time of.

whisper When you whisper, you say something very quietly.

Ernie has to **whisper** **while** the Pigeon News is on.

whistle A whistle is something that makes a loud, shrill sound when air is blown through it.

whistle When you whistle, you make a loud, shrill sound by blowing air through your lips in a special way.

Sully likes to **whistle** while he works.

who Who is a word used to ask questions or talk about people.

whole The whole of something is all the parts of it together.

whose Whose is a word used to ask questions or talk about things that belong to people.

why Why is a word used to ask or talk about the reason for something.

wide How wide something is means how far it is from one side to the other. When something is wide, it is not narrow.

wife A wife is a woman who is married.

will If you will do something, you are going to do it.

win When you win a game or a race, you finish ahead of the others.

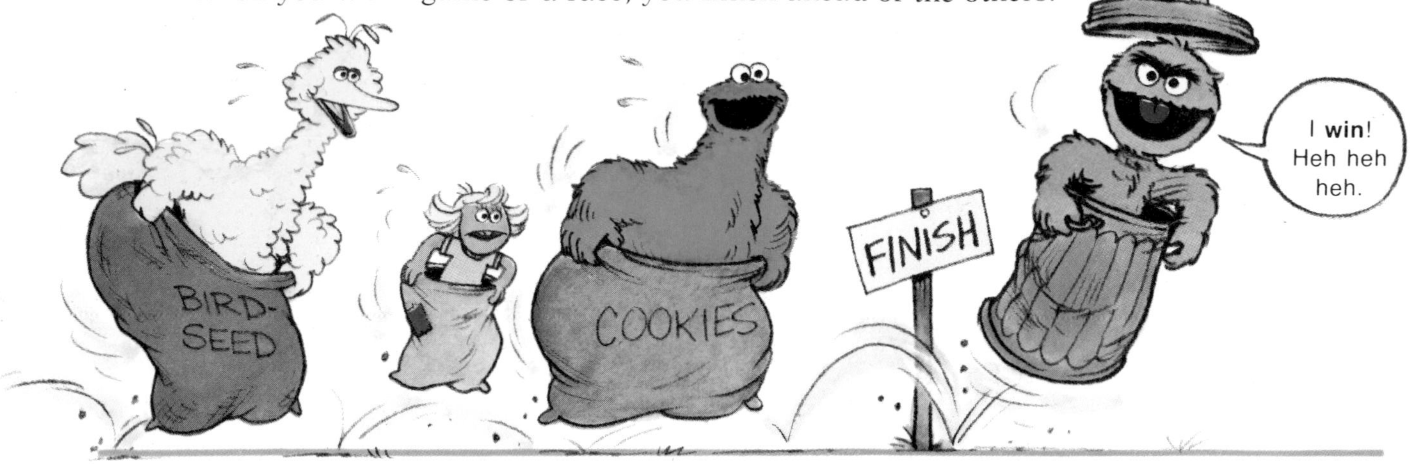
BIRD-SEED
COOKIES
FINISH
I **win**! Heh heh heh.

wind Wind is air that is moving.

The **wind** can make this toy pinwheel turn around.
The **wind** can make this flag wave.
Oops! The **wind** just blew my hat away.

window A window is an opening in a building or a vehicle to let in air or light. Most windows have glass in them.

Bert is looking out the **window.**

wing A wing is the part of birds, bats, and some insects that helps them fly. Airplanes also have wings.

My airplane has two **wings.**
All birds have two **wings.**
But some birds cannot fly.

winter Winter is the name of a season. Winter comes after fall.

wish A wish is something that you hope will come true. When you wish for something, you want it.

witch A witch is a person with magical powers. Many fairy tales have witches in them.

Connie the **witch** is reading a story.

with With means using or having. With also means in the company of.

woman A woman is a grown-up girl.

There is one **woman,** one girl, and one monster in the elevator.

wonder When you wonder about something, you would like to know about it.

wonderful Something wonderful is surprising or amazing. Sometimes the word wonderful is used to mean very good.

That's **wonderful**!

wood Wood is the hard part of a tree. Many things are made of wood.

I like to build things with **wood.**

word A word is a group of letters or sounds that has a meaning. You can say a word or read it.

There are so many **words** that begin with W. WOW!

work When you work, you do something that uses energy. Most people work at jobs to earn money.

I **work** at the post office.
U.S. MAIL
Special
I **work** at the grocery store.
I **work** at the hospital.
I **work** at the factory.
I **work** at school.
MATH
I am not **working.** I am resting.

world A world is a planet. Our world is the planet earth.

I can see the whole **world** from my little spaceship.

worm A worm is a tiny animal with a long, soft body and no legs. Earthworms live under the ground.

Slimey is my pet **worm.**

worry When you worry, you are afraid that something bad is going to happen.

Be careful, Ernie! Those cups are going to fall.
You **worry** too much, Bert.

wrap When you wrap something, you cover it.

I have to **wrap** this present for Mr. Snuffle-upagus.

write When you write, you put words on something—usually paper.

writer A writer is someone who writes stories, letters, or other things for people to read.

Herry is a **writer.** Does he **write** with his left hand or his right hand?
I **write** with a pencil.

wrong When something is wrong, it is not correct. It is not true.

Farley has four apples. Right or **wrong**?
Wrong! I have only three apples.

I wonder where the words wart, weed, whimper, and whine went.

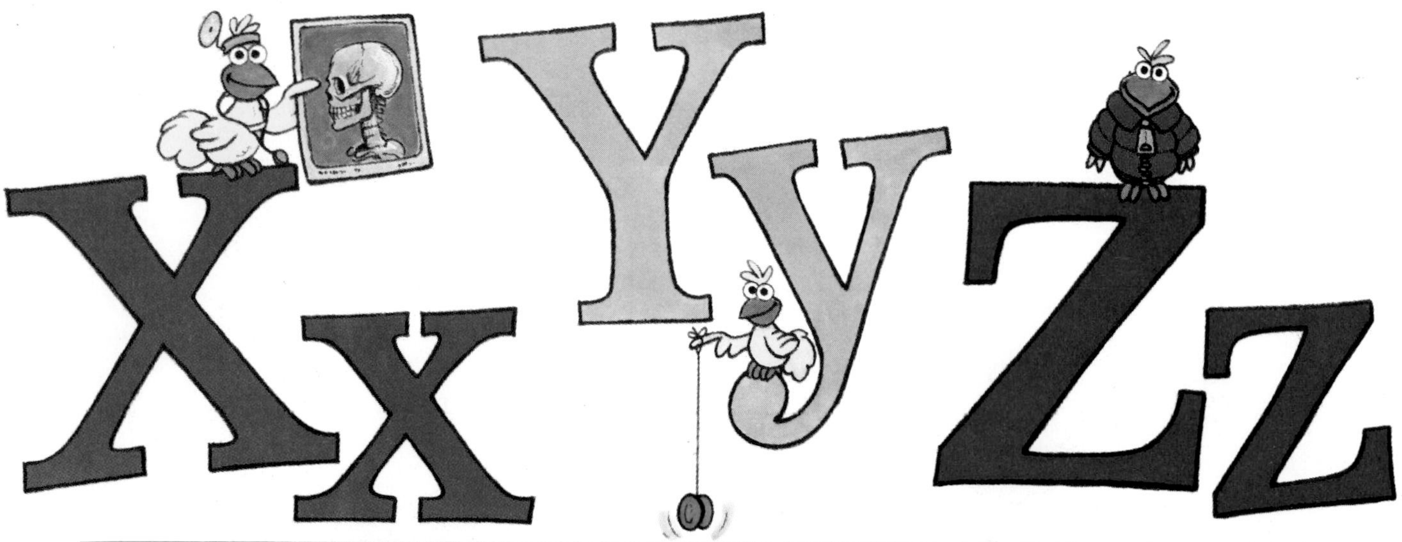

A B C D E F G H I J K L M N O P Q R S T U V W X Y Z

x-ray An x-ray is a picture of the inside of something. Sometimes the doctor takes an x-ray of your body to see if anything is wrong inside.

The doctor took an **x-ray** of Mr. Hooper's chest.

xylophone A xylophone is a musical instrument with two rows of wooden bars that you hit with wooden hammers.

Frazzle likes to play the **xylophone.**

yard A yard is a piece of ground next to a house or a school or another kind of building.

Biff and Sully are building a fence around their **yard.**

yawn When you yawn, you open your mouth wide and take a deep breath. You yawn because you are tired or bored.

YAWN!
And I found this bottle cap on the sidewalk one day when I was walking home from the store. I had just bought some oatmeal . . . .

Bert's stories make Ernie **yawn.**

year A year is an amount of time that is three hundred and sixty-five days long. A new year begins with January and ends with December. Look up the word calendar.

Today is my birthday. Now I will have to wait a whole **year** for my next birthday.

yell When you yell, you cry out loudly.

Cookie Monster **yells** KOWABUNGA when he sees a pile of cookies.

yes Yes is a word you use to say that something is true. You can also use yes to say you will or can do something.

Cookie Monster, do you want a cookie?
YES!

yesterday Yesterday is the day that came before today.

Yesterday I washed the clothes.
Today I am ironing them.

you You means the person or persons spoken to.

This belongs to **you**, Ernie.
These belong to **you**, Bert.

young Someone who is young has lived a short time. A young person has not lived as long as someone who is old.

Farley is **young**, but his baby brother is **younger.** Their grandfather is old.

your Your is another way of saying belonging to you.

yours When something belongs to you, it is yours.

yourself Yourself is sometimes used instead of you.

Yo-Yo™ A Yo-Yo is a toy that goes up and down on a string.

Betty Lou is trying to win the **Yo-Yo** contest.

zebra A zebra is a white animal with black stripes. A zebra has four legs, a mane, and a tail.

zipper A zipper is something that is used to fasten clothes or other things.

zoo A zoo is a place where animals are kept so that people can see them.

Big Bird likes to visit the animals at the **zoo.**

Aa Bb Cc
Dd Ee
Ff Gg Hh
Ii Jj Kk
Ll Mm